Rikhia

WORLD YOGA CONVENTION 2013
GANGA DARSHAN, MUNGER, BIHAR, INDIA
23rd–27th October 2013

Rikhia

The Vision of a Sage

From the teachings of Swami Satyananda Saraswati

Yoga Publications Trust, Munger, Bihar, India

© Sivananda Math 2012

All rights reserved. No part of this publication may be reproduced, transmitted or stored in a retrieval system, in any form or by any means, without permission in writing from Yoga Publications Trust.

The terms Satyananda Yoga® and Bihar Yoga® are registered trademarks owned by International Yoga Fellowship Movement (IYFM). The use of the same in this book is with permission and should not in any way be taken as affecting the validity of the marks.

Published by Yoga Publications Trust
   First edition 2012

ISBN: 978-93-81620-29-8

Publisher and distributor: Yoga Publications Trust, Ganga Darshan, Munger, Bihar, India.

Website: www.biharyoga.net

Printed at Aegean Offset Printers, Greater Noida

Dedication

*In humility we offer this dedication to
Swami Sivananda Saraswati, who initiated
Swami Satyananda Saraswati into the secrets of yoga.*

Contents

Introduction 1
1. God's Mandate 9
2. Rikhia: Blessed Abode 23
3. My Neighbours 39
4. Village Development 63
5. People Development 115
6. Education 158
7. Health 180
8. Marriage 186
9. Prasad 200

Glossary 242

There is a voice that comes from the depth of my soul saying that I should live in a remote village amongst people who are illiterate, poor and unhappy, and serve them. I have decided that I will follow my call. I will leave whenever I receive Gurudeva's blessings.

—*Swami Satyananda*
4 March, 1956, Rishikesh

Just as I spread yoga throughout the world, I will donate cows to each and every house. Each house will have a water supply. There will be fields to till. I shall see to it that this happens: 'Green Rikhia, Prosperous Rikhia.' This is my promise and my pledge to you.

—Swami Satyananda
3 December, 1996, Rikhiapeeth

1

God's Mandate

God showed me this place. He told me to come here. He told me to do panchagni, the sacrifice of the five fires, and He said, "Love your neighbours as I have loved you, provide them with the same facilities which I have provided for you."

It is strange that I came to Rikhia, leaving all other places. Even though this place is so close to Munger, I had never thought of staying here. I am, and have always been, a man of resources. So why stay here in Rikhia? I did not choose this place. God has given me this place. After I left Munger in 1988, when I was in seclusion in Tryambakeshwar, near Nasik, I heard God's command and was shown this place very clearly. I came here and started following His instructions. Here, my eyes have opened further because this is a beautiful place, a great and powerful place. Listen to what I am telling you. Understand it plainly and in a straightforward manner. I am not talking symbolically. I have been sent here for a specific purpose. I am telling you the facts and you should understand them as facts. I heard God one day, just as you are hearing me right now.

I came to realize we are dependent on grace, after practising spiritual life, sannyasa life, for many years. I tried everything possible. I had spent more than sixty years in sadhana. There is no sadhana that I have not done at one time or another in my life, but not once did my number come up in the lottery. However, after coming to Rikhia, luck smiled upon me and I got the winning number. On 19th January 1983, I resigned from the institution. I said, "God, I am tired. I can't do anything more. I have always wanted to go very high in spiritual life. I wanted to attain this and that, but now I am tired." In August 1988, I left everything: the work, responsibilities, friends, disciples, money and everything that I could consider to be my accomplishments. I could not decide what to do. I went to Varanasi, then to Vindhyachal. I went to Maihar and then to Pashupatinath.

Promise fulfilled

After travelling to practically all the holy places in India, I finally went to Tryambakeshwar, near Nasik. Tryambakeshwar is thirty kilometres from Nasik, from where the Godavari River emerges and flows eastward. There, on 14th July 1989, I sought darshan of the jyotirlingam of my ishta deva, Mahamrityunjaya. There and then, I surrendered. I laid down all my arms as a defeated soldier: I wanted amnesty from God. Before going to Munger in 1963, I had been to my ishta, Lord Mrityunjaya, when I had made a promise to him. Since then, he had given me whatever I asked of him, I said, "I came to you in 1963 with a request. You fulfilled it. I gave you a promise and I am fulfilling it. Now tell me what to do and I promise hereafter I will do what you tell me. I will not do anything on my own."

It was the monsoon season and sannyasins are not supposed to move around for a minimum of two months during Chaturmas, the four months of rains. I had never followed that rule, this was the first time that I had decided to do it. I acquired a small room there, 8' x 8', in a *goshala*, a cowshed. I had a small mat, a little pressure stove, filtered water and a small cane stand. I did not eat anything. I would get one litre of milk in the morning and

that is all I had. I would boil it three times a day, in the morning, at midday and at night. On 14th July 1989, in the evening, I remember it well; I sat down and said, "Lord, I have come. All my duties are over. I am empty and, so to say, unemployed. What should I do next? I want your guidance!" I was alone.

God's first command

In the middle of the night, a storm began. There was torrential rain and lightning, outside and inside, both! Then I heard a very clear, shrill voice say, "Twenty-one thousand six hundred times." That's all, nothing else. So, what was the meaning of this shrill voice that came in the night?

I understood what it meant, because this was what I had been teaching. In one minute, we normally breathe fifteen times. In one hour, with natural, spontaneous breathing, not pranayama, we all breathe nine hundred times. In twenty-four hours, we breathe twenty-one thousand, six hundred times. Therefore, the instruction was clear. For twenty-four hours, do not eat, do not go to the toilet, do not sleep, do not yawn, only be aware of your natural breath. Do not interfere with your breathing; just watch the natural breath for twenty-four hours. I started the sadhana from that day. It was no joke and I realized it after coming here to Rikhia.

The next thing I needed to know was where to live, because that goshala was not a permanent place. I had asked to stay there for two months only. Munger was my previous incarnation so I did not want to go back there. I could have had a very good cave in Gangotri, the source of the Ganga in the Himalayas, where a helicopter could have just dropped all my things from Delhi. It would not have been at all difficult for me. I could have even taken wood to Rishikesh by helicopter to build a kutir. My guru's ashram in Rishikesh is very big. There, I could easily have had a plot of land. Swami Sivananda had once told me to buy land and build a hut there, but I was not in favour of Rishikesh because of the crowds; from Delhi people can go immediately to Rishikesh. It is difficult to get to Rikhia and a person seldom has the courage to come twice.

The third option was Mount Abu. Near Mount Abu there is a nice place, called Guru Shikhar where the footprints of Dattatreya, and a temple of Atri and Anasuya can be found. I was offered a place at Mount Abu, but I did not stay there because there was not a plentiful supply of water. I had been told to stay somewhere where there was a plentiful supply of water, and if there was no water I should leave. The first necessity of a paramahamsa is water, the second is wind, the third is earth and the fourth is sun. One does not want to stay in a place where these necessities are lacking. Therefore, I do not want to stay in the city.

The second command

On 8th September 1989, on the birthday of my guru, I woke at about two o'clock in the early morning, made a little tea, took my bath and sat down. I gradually lost consciousness. There was a huge storm with lightning and thunder. This storm happened internally, not externally. My mind sank again. There was total quiet, and I remember there was moonlight, as you have on the tenth or the eleventh day before the full moon. At 4 am the shrill voice came again, saying, "Chitabhoomi." *Chitabhoomi* means cremation ground. That was all, burial ground. *Chita* means burning of the body and *bhoomi* means ground.

The question in my mind had been, "Where am I going to stay?" At once, I understood the meaning of what I had heard; it was a clear instruction that I was to go to a cremation ground. In India, in the vedic mythology and in the Puranas, particularly the *Shiva Purana*, there are references to two cremation grounds. One is at Varanasi, known as Shiva's shmashana bhoomi. The other is this entire area of Deoghar which, in our scriptures, is referred to as Sati's chitabhoomi. When the voice uttered the word 'chitabhoomi', He meant this place, and I also saw this property very clearly in a vision, the building, the trees, everything as clearly as on a television screen.

At about seven o'clock that day, Swami Satsangi arrived from Munger with prasad and I described to her what I had seen. I said to her, "You don't have to stay here. Go back immediately. I have seen a place near Deoghar. Please go there and find it." I didn't have to worry, I just told Swami Satsangi, "That is the kind of place where I have to go, so please ask Swami Niranjan if he can arrange it for me. I'll go and stay there."

She went by taxi to Mumbai, and then flew to Patna and from Patna to Deoghar. She phoned Swami Niranjan and told him that she had found this place, which belonged to a local businessman. The businessman had intended to set up a stone crusher here, but could not, as the villagers objected to the pollution it would cause to the local environment. On the very same day, 8th September, the owner had also decided to sell this property. So, He tells me to go there, and He tells him to sell. This is not a coincidence. I have had many occurrences like this in my life.

Swami Satsangi went to Deoghar, and on the 10th she was shown this land. She phoned Swami Niranjan and the property was negotiated that same day. They went to Kolkata because the local courts were on strike. In Kolkata, they made the title deed, the deed of ownership, according to the Transfer Deed Act. The title was struck on the 12th, and on the 14th, I received the news that the property had been acquired and I could leave Tryambakeshwar. Then I came here. In just four days, the property was in our hands although I was far away in the south-west of India. Things happen on their own. It took one full year to negotiate and acquire the transfer of a second property on the other side of the road, despite living here for over a year and the villagers wanting to transfer it to us.

When I came to this place there was nothing growing here; it was barren. I arrived here on 23rd September 1989, at twelve o'clock, midday. It was the day of the vernal equinox when everything is in perfect balance; day and night are both exactly twelve hours long. On such a day, I set foot here at exactly midday. Was that auspicious moment a coincidence? That day, I was standing over there with a few people, including some of the locals; I did not know where to put the *dhuni*, the sadhana fireplace. I was standing here when suddenly a twelve-foot-long serpent appeared at that spot, and it then circumambulated the entire property. Then I said, "I shall light the dhuni here." When God gives His command, you have to tune in and be able to understand. Things become so easy that you do not have to think or struggle. When it is God's will, everything is easy. When it is man's will, then you have to struggle. You can only attune to God's command when you stop thinking. God gave the command and so it happened that way.

The ultimate mandate

I came here to Rikhia and pitched my tent. Then I made a small grass hut, a *parna kutir*, to live in. I closed all the doors and made a sankalpa that I would do *panchagni sadhana*, the sadhana of five fires. When I started this sadhana, Swami Satsangi, who is the *karobari*, the caretaker, was in a big dilemma. Every day she would say, "What kind of life do these people live here? I can't understand it and I can't accept it." I said, "What am I going to do?" She also did not know what to do. So, a year passed and then another one. During that period of panchagni, in my third year here, I started an additional sadhana, *purascharana*, observance

of the repetition of mantra, of my ishta mantra. I took a sankalpa to complete purascharana of one hundred and eight lakh mantras, ten million and eight hundred thousand mantras, 10,800,000. This meant three hundred days of mantra repetition at the rate of eight to ten hours a day, quite a heavy schedule. That year I did not meet anyone; I was in total seclusion and isolation. I used to sit in the Akhara and do my mantra. It was a lovely year.

Some time after I had completed the purascharana, the shrill voice came again, "Take care of your neighbours as I have taken care of you." That is all. This was not an idea. This was God's mandate. It was not a hallucination. It was a mandate and I heard it very clearly! I do not experience strange psychological states. I am a perfectly normal person, but that set me reflecting on His words. I told myself, "Satyananda, are you very selfish? Will you eat all the sweets yourself? Will you have the darshan of God all by yourself? What is the use of the atmajnana that you attain? How can the world benefit by your spiritual gain and self-realization? You are very selfish, give up selfishness." I said to God, "Show me the path. I am blind. Tell me what to do. To give them clothes is not enough. Money is not enough; money cannot buy love. I cannot purchase love and give it to somebody." Thenceforth, God began to show me the path. He said, "Give blankets to those who are fighting the cold." In this way, slowly the guidance came in clear terms.

Of course, the definition of neighbour may change later; it may not be just Rikhia or Deoghar. That depends upon my capacity. Those who say, "This is mine and that is thine" belong to the lower category, but for people who are generous, openhearted and broadminded, the whole world is one family, even though it may be split into many different countries. I spoke to Swami Niranjan, Swami Satsangi and Swami Vedananda, a German swami. They said, "That is a very good idea." I have a small kutir. That is the facility my God has provided me with. I will provide others with the same facility, because He has ordered it.

I am His servant

He gave His mandate and it is going to happen. I do not even worry about how it will happen. If I have the feeling that I am a servant, I do not have to worry. The servant does not have to worry. He just has to carry out his orders. A servant has no accountability, no responsibility. He just has to do his duty and not think too much. I do not have to be anxious or worried. If He gives me an order I will do it, then things become easy. Whatever I do here is because I have been told to do it by somebody whom you do not know, whom I have never seen and whose phone number I do not have. He has asked me to do it and since hearing this message, every time I sit down, it comes to my mind.

I am doing it because He asked me to. So now, to live only for others should be the dharma of Swami Satyananda's life. Since the day this thought came to my mind, I have achieved the aim for which I left my home, fifty or sixty years ago. I did tantra, sadhana, I did everything. I read a lot, travelled around the whole world, saw all the temples of Christians, Muslims, Iranians and Parsis, but now I have received His order and I am meant to work for others, not for my own spiritual salvation. I have told myself, "Satyananda, now you are a nobody. You are neither a guru nor a disciple." Since His mandate, whatever I do is not with the idea of achieving realization, salvation, moksha, emancipation, kaivalya, or nirvikalpa samadhi.

Lakshmi's support

I do not worry about money; I do not even think about it. I have never had to think about money in my life. Fish never think about water. Do fish get thirsty? Lakshmi is my mother and she gave me a blank chequebook. Whenever I want to, I sign a cheque and give it to those who need it. Lakshmi has assured me, "Swami Satyananda, if you do as I tell you and spend this money for others, my bank is open for you. The day you use this money for your personal enjoyment, the cheque will bounce." This is absolutely true. She told

me, "Satyananda, as long as you are not amassing wealth for your own comfort and luxury you will get whatever you want. I'll be with you." Of course, I am not a spendthrift. I said, "I am a good son. I will not use your money for my personal enjoyment and luxury. I will only use it for those who need it." Be it the earthquake in Bhuj or the Orissa catastrophe, I can spend as much as I like on relief measures for disaster-affected people. That divine gift is always there for me. It is a service to the nation.

Our swamis do not need to live on alms; they are resourceful people. If need be, we can drive taxis and earn money. I also know all the ways and have never had any problem with money. One day, a lady from the neighbourhood came asking for five or six hundred rupees. Her house had burned down and she wanted some relief. I said, "No, we will not give cash. After the rains are over, we will build a house for her." Her house was the first one we constructed. Her family members are cobblers by caste. Then the second, third and fourth houses were constructed.

Effort, planning and dedication

In the meantime, our sannyasins have been trained. A swami from Orissa builds the houses. Another swami from France knows how to make bricks and is in charge of the brick kiln. We produce hundreds of thousands of bricks here, for which we get coal from Dhanbad. The government has permitted us to collect all the sand that we need for our work. We have been provided with a lorry and a tractor and we pick up sand from the riverbed. We make the bricks here and get the *puwal*, straw for the roofs from the local villagers. There are good engineers in Deoghar who provide us with free designs for low-cost village housing.

There are other things to bear in mind as God's mandate unfolds and the work evolves, as good work also requires effort, imagination and planning. Even as bad work needs planning and effort, good work needs more planning and more hard work. To take on four houses at one time is not easy. I have enough resources to make about two hundred houses in a month. Sivananda Math is the institution that does this work, not Bihar School of Yoga. I have two wings: Bihar School of Yoga is one wing and Sivananda Math is another. They are my wings, right and left.

The Bihar School of Yoga spreads God's name through meditation, concentration, asanas, pranayama, mudra and bandha. Sivananda Math spreads God's name through selfless service. Both wings are necessary and must be steady. These wings are both very useful, very rich institutions; they are not your average institutions. However, they need dedicated and imaginative staff. During the construction of Tribhuvan, this three-storey building, an Australian swami, Nirmalratna, would stand there day and night supervising. Once she became dehydrated, once she had conjunctivitis, but she stood by it. Swami Atmamuktananda drives the truck and the tractor and brings sand from the riverbed. Here, women operate everything; they are trained for every work. I told them, "If you want to serve in any capacity, I have faith in you." I have no definition of right or wrong, good or bad. If you work for the good of others, therein lies your goodness.

Our women here have great confidence and can go anywhere by day or night. I do not need to watch over them.

Whatever they do is their responsibility. When our French swami went to Patna, initially I sent someone with her for security. She is a pretty girl; anyone could fall for her. Now she goes alone. Until and unless I have faith in her, she cannot develop a strong character. In the same way, the village parents should put trust in their children. Only then will the children develop character. Women here drive the tractor to plough fields even thirty miles away. Women do everything here. There is no distinction between men and women and the local women notice this.

Serving others

Soon, about ten thousand villagers will receive blankets; school children will receive bicycles; cricket teams will receive cricket bats and balls; little children will receive games, and young girls going to their husband's house will receive ornaments, sindoor, mangalsutra, beautiful Bangalore saris, chappals, brassieres and everything they will need. Why not? I will provide them with the same facilities that God has provided for me. I will love them as He has loved me, because He has helped me. Love does not mean anything else. When you serve others, you feel satisfaction, you sleep well, and you have good thoughts, good feelings and a good mental state. What more do you want? It is a pleasure which cannot be explained or expressed. When you do good to others, when you work for others and not for yourself, it brings immense joy, *ananda,* bliss. This is what is happening here.

If you only live for yourself and your family, you cannot be absolutely happy. You and your family are just nothing in this universe. When you and your family live for others, only then does your life have meaning. When you live only for others, then you are really great. God will definitely shower his blessings and grace on you: *Paropakaaraaya sataam vibhootaya* – "The virtues of the noble and great are for the good of others." Trees do not eat their fruit. Does an apple tree eat its own apples? Do rivers drink their own water?

That is called 'doing good to others', without expectation. If your mind is patterned along that line, then every meditation leads to greater harmony. Every meditation will give you blessings. Otherwise, you smell like a toilet. You can put on perfume and smell nice outside, but underneath there is the smell of a toilet. With a selfish, limited, crooked mind, you are trying to smell better by putting on artificial perfumes. This will not work until you have shaped your life in the mould of selfless service as far as possible.

I wish to emphasize one point. The tendency to collect and amass property gives rise to wrong conduct; it leads to undesirable thought processes and unholy attitudes. However, the tendency to sacrifice brings about a complete change in man's behaviour, his way of thinking, his way of living, and his way of expression. If you fill a bottle with water and do not use it, the water putrefies. If the water continues to flow, it never putrefies. This is the statement of our sages and seers. This should be the attitude of human behaviour.

Luck and chances are nothing but the right and proper use of opportunities which come in the way of every person. Golden opportunities come in everyone's life at some point or the other, even if only for a short time. No man has been born without these opportunities. He who understands this and makes the best use of them can become a good athlete, a great scholar, or a famous soldier. He can change his destiny. This is relevant.

My promise, pledge and duty
Now, you have the opportunity to change your destiny. Swami Satyananda, who has spread yoga throughout the world, will get the work done but I will not do it myself. My business is with God. However, it is my duty to inspire you all. At present, the resources and the workers are here, but the problem is: *Ayam nijah, paroveti* – "This is mine, that is his." Those people who think like this have narrow minds. Help them as I have helped you.

The sum and substance of what I have said is that we were born through the grace of God, not through the grace of our fathers. We live by the grace of God. There is nothing beyond that. It is by the grace of God that we have started thinking about spiritual life and about how to improve the quality of our life in general. It is through the grace of God that things happen in our life, both good and bad. Remember this!

Just as I spread yoga throughout the world, here in Rikhia I will donate cows to each and every house. Each house will have a water supply. There will be fields to till. I shall see to it that God's mandate is fulfilled. Green Rikhia, prosperous Rikhia. This is my promise and my pledge to you.

2

Rikhia: Blessed Abode

DEOGHAR – A SPIRITUAL CENTRE

Geographically, Deoghar is located in the southeast of Bihar, now Jharkhand. It is a land of the Santhalis. Just as there are different tribes in Madhya Pradesh, similarly, the native tribe of Deoghar is Santhali. The Santhalis are simple and nice people. They have a great culture, greater than ours. Their king was not a Santhali; he was a follower of vedic religion, like Rama, Krishna, Harish Chandra and others. The population consists mainly of *pandas* or priests, Santhalis and Bengalis. The pandas were brought here from Mithila by the royal family of Giddaur (Bihar) to conduct the *pooja*, worship, for Lord Shiva. Deoghar was once a vast forest. Its only inhabitants were a tribal race known as Santhals, and the entire district was called Santhal Parganas.

Historically, Deoghar, which is also known as Baidyanath Dham, finds mention in the *Shiva Purana* which dates it back to the Treta Yuga, the era of Lord Rama and Ravana. More recent history dates its development to two hundred years ago when the British first came here. There are several towns named after the British commissioners who were deputed here, and their aristocratic bungalows still remain. The British liked this place. Here they could find respite from the terrible heat of Bihar, and there was ample opportunity for them to indulge in the sport of hunting. It is said that tigers, leopards, elephants and boars roamed freely in the dense jungles of Deoghar.

In 1983, Deoghar was declared as an independent district. The land is undulating and surrounded by hills. Gradually the Santhals began clearing the jungles for the cultivation of crops, and later Bengalis came in large numbers to settle here, acquiring land from the Santhals at throwaway prices. It is said that during the World War II, Marwaris too came here from Kolkata and built vast mansions to keep their jewels and money safe in underground vaults. These houses still exist, although in a dilapidated condition. There are also several big institutions here: Ramakrishna Mission, Hindi Vidya Peeth, Balanand Brahmachari Ashram, and they are reputable institutions.

The name *Deoghar*, which literally means 'home of the gods', is a modern name. In Sanskrit works we find in its place Hridaya peeth, Ravana-vana, Ketaki-vana, Haritaki-vana and Vaidyanatha. The sanctity of Baidyanath is mentioned in several authentic works on pilgrimages dating from the 12th to the 14th century AD. Authentic portions of the Puranas also refer to it, and as they are unquestionably anterior to the 10th century, Baidyanath must have attained considerable celebrity even in those times.

Deoghar is a spiritual town, an awakened town, not a commercial one. It is a great pilgrim centre, and religious saints and sadhus come here in large numbers. Moreover, one visit to the large and magnificent Baidyanath temple here is sufficient to convince anyone that this seat of Lord Shiva is a powerhouse of energy. Sage Narada, in his description of Baidyanath Dham to Hanuman, describes it as the only place where Lord Shiva grants boons to each and every person, whether deserving or undeserving, sinner or saint.

At one time, Deoghar was the base of siddhas, nagas, tantrics and aghoras who practised sadhana here in large numbers. Nowadays their presence has reduced greatly, perhaps due to the fact that those sects have degenerated

a great deal. It is a strong belief here that a fake sadhu, or one who practises sadhana for the wrong reasons, will be driven out for some reason or other by the power of Baba Baidyanath. Belief in His omnipresence is so strong amongst people and omnipresent He is!

As well as a seat for one of the twelve jyotirlingams of Lord Shiva, another unique but little-known fact about Deoghar is that, apart from being a Shiva sthana, it is also a very important siddha shaktipeeth. People from Nepal to Kanyakumari come to pay their respects and ask for their wishes to be fulfilled here. Deoghar is the cremation ground of Sati, the consort of Shiva and, therefore, it has great importance. After Kamakhya, it is considered to be the second tantric seat of Devi.

Some Puranas ascribe the advent of Baidyanath Dham at Deoghar to the Satya Yuga, or the first age of the world. It is said that when Sati immolated herself at the yajna of her father in defiance of his disrespect to her husband, Shiva became furious. Carrying the body of Sati on his shoulders, he raged across the worlds. Lord Vishnu, seeing the uncontrollable grief and rage that had overcame Shiva, sent forth his *sudarshan chakra*, discus, to dismember her dead body. It was cut into sixty-four pieces, and as Shiva roamed the length and breadth of the universe in wild abandon, different parts of Sati's body fell in different places, which became the sixty-four *peethas*, or important places for worship, of Shakti. Her heart fell at Baidyanath Dham and this is known as the *Hridayapeeth*. It is on this very spot that the jyotirlinga was later established. Thus, both Shiva and Shakti are eternally present here. Every day, first arati and pooja are offered to Devi and then the doors of Baba Baidyanath temple are opened.

The people in Deoghar have one great quality which deserves praise: a high regard for sadhus and sannyasins. They take a keen interest in the worshippers, devotees of God, saints and great souls who come here for satsang. This you will not find elsewhere. Even in places like Rishikesh and Haridwar, you will find a lot of disorder in this regard. Things have become topsy-turvy there, but here it is not like that. If the electricity department is asked to provide electricity for satsang, the power has to come from Patna if it is not available here. The Deoghar electrician must sit in the Patna electric supply office to see that the power supply to this place is not disrupted. If anything goes out of order, he has to rectify the fault. The required facilities are provided at any cost because it is the right of this town to hold satsang. Those facilities will not be given to businessmen or for running iron factories, but they will be provided here because satsang is taking place.

A twenty-five volt transformer was previously installed and now it is being replaced with a sixty volt one. The capacity has been increased because the requirement here has increased. The transformer belongs to the government. They take great care of us. The business class cooperates fully with us. The owners of the different local hotels also cooperate with us. We do not have any problems here.

BAIDYANATH DHAM

Here in Deoghar, there is a very ancient Shiva temple called Baidyanath Dham. The word *baidya* means 'doctor', *nath* means 'chief'. Baba Baidyanath heals the ills of life. While you are here, you must have darshan of Baidyanath Dham; you will find Shiva, the ishta devata of the whole state of Bihar.

The reason for the popularity of Baidyanath temple is very simple. It is a temple of the people; the trustees are only the managers. A trust was established for the management and upkeep of the temple. When a government trust is set up, a membership has to be formed. There are many routine jobs which are entrusted to the local people, like ringing the bell, cleaning, making wicks for the ghee and oil lamps, cooking prasad, making flower garlands for the Lord, making thread for the garlands and playing the drums. There are cobblers who make the drums. All these people go and work in the temple, but they do not receive salaries. They receive their due share from the annual earnings of the temple. All the people from the village have a share in the

temple. Suppose the annual earning is a few lakhs or even a crore, a certain percentage will go into a reserve fund and the rest will be distributed among the local workers, according to the standard practice. The same system prevails at the Badrinath Temple in the Himalayas.

Open to all

Hygienically, you may consider Baidyanath Dham as dirty, but spiritually it is very powerful. There are two aspects: the hygienic and the spiritual. Some take the hygienic aspect into consideration, but it is the spiritual that is more important. Baidyanath Dham is the only ancient temple to which non-Hindus can go. This temple does not concern itself with religion and everyone can visit; there is no discrimination. People of all religions, whether Hindu, Christian, Muslim, can enter here. Foreigners are not stopped from entering either, as they are in some other tirthas. The temple is open to all, no matter to which caste, creed or religion they belong. Our Miyaji and his wife Khatoon, a Muslim couple who supply food for my dog Bholenath, go to Baidyanath Dham. When I ask them where they have been, they reply that they have been for Baba's darshan. The priests have not made any rules of exclusion. However, when the abhisheka or shringara rituals are on, the door is closed for some time and nobody is allowed in.

Origin of Baba Baidyanath

The central figure around which everything revolves here is of course Baba Baidyanath. Carved out of a single rock, its magnificence and power draw lakhs of people to Deoghar for worship. A curious fact is that unlike other jyotirlingas, the black stone slab which forms the jyotirlinga is slightly depressed and the actual linga is absent. The current story is that due to the rubbing of the stone by devotees during worship, the linga has become concave, but the ancient story is different. Ravana, the famed demon king of the *Ramayana*, who also happened to be a great scholar and accomplished yogi, was returning to Lanka from Mount Kailash where he had acquired a boon from Shiva, after performing austere tapasya for a long period. The boon he received was a jyotirlinga which he was taking back to install at Lanka so that Lord Shiva, his ishta devata, would be eternally present there. However, Lord Shiva placed one condition on Ravana before he gave the linga. He instructed that this linga should never be put down on the ground en route to Lanka, or else it would not be possible to remove it again. To this Ravana agreed and set off on his journey.

Now all the devas, including Lord Vishnu, became apprehensive about Ravana acquiring such a great power as the jyotirlinga of Lord Shiva in Lanka. They, therefore, connived to prevent him in some way or the other. Varuna entered his body, on account of which Ravana felt an extreme urge to urinate. He stopped, and seeing a young brahmin boy standing nearby, gave the boy the linga to hold, instructing him not to put it down until he returned. Ravana took a long time and the boy, who they say was Lord Vishnu himself, put the linga down whereupon it sank into the ground. On his return, Ravana found to his dismay that no matter how hard he tried, the stone would not move an inch. When Ravana was unable to lift the linga off the ground, he rammed his fist into it in anger and frustration, causing a depression in the stone. So it stayed there, and the place where it all happened was Deoghar. This is why the place is also called as Ravaneshwar Baidyanath. The spot where Ravana came down to earth is identified with the present Harlajori Mandir; the place where the lingam was deposited is now Deoghar, and the jyotirlinga of Shiva itself is known as Baba Baidyanath.

Baidyanath Dham is a Santhali temple, but the Ganga water for abhisheka of the linga is brought from Sultanganj, which is outside Santhali jurisdiction. This is regarded as a symbol of unity, because Sultanganj falls within the territory of Anga. People bring the Ganga water from there and offer it here.

Baidyanath yatra

Perhaps the most significant feature of Baba Baidyanath Dham which deserves special mention is the annual Kanwariya mela held in the month of Shravan, July. This is believed to be a highly auspicious time for darshan of Baba Baidyanath, bathing the jyotirlinga with Ganga water, offering flowers and bael leaves, and praying to Shiva. So ingrained is this belief, that during the monsoon in month of Shravan, crores of devotees walk barefoot from Sultanganj, one hundred kilometres away, carrying Ganga *jala*, water, in their gourds or earthen pots on a bamboo pole, known as a *kanwar*. The water is collected from Sultanganj, as it is the closest spot to Deoghar where the Ganga flows. At Sultanganj, the Ganga reverses and flows north, like in Munger, so it is an auspicious place. With great care, the pilgrims carry the kanwar on their shoulders through the winding paths, chanting *Bol Bam, Bol Bam, Bol Bam, Bol Bam!* all the way to their destination. The pilgrims observe strict rules throughout the journey and are not permitted to place the kanwar on the ground at any point on this journey from Sultanganj to Baba Baidyanath. This is perhaps symbolic of Ravana's mistake in putting Shiva's jyotirlinga on the ground.

This pilgrimage is an old tradition. It takes the pilgrims three to five days to reach this place and during these days, they dress like sadhus and live like sannyasins. They are householders from different strata of society: king and subject alike, rich and poor, politicians and officers, old and young, men and women, happy, unhappy, as well as people suffering mentally and physically. There are no religious barriers; Christians, Buddhists and Hindus, anyone can make this journey. They all make the pilgrimage from Sultanganj to Baidyanath Dham. When they arrive in Deoghar, they enter the temple and pour all the Ganga water they have carried on to Lord Shiva, Baba Baidyanath.

Some pilgrims also prostrate at every step of the journey. Doing namaskara, they prostrate on the road and pray with each step throughout the one hundred kilometres until they reach the temple. It takes a long time; maybe a few months for them to reach here. That is austerity, or *tapasya*, perhaps it is like purgatory! People suffering from incurable diseases take this observance. Man has made so many mistakes in his lifetime. In order to eliminate the karma, he undertakes many forms of austerity and this is one of them. This type of austerity, which is known as *prayaschitta*, is a part of the vedic dharma, and it is found in Christianity as well.

There are many rich people who walk on that road from Sultanganj. As they are affluent, they send their servants ahead by car with cooking items, bedding and other necessities. When they arrive at the resting place, the servants are already there cooking, and the beds are ready. The entire road becomes a walking street for that one month. Rich or poor, all have to walk as well as practice self-restraint, or *sanyam*, for that period. The diet has to be sattwic without onions or garlic. The yatris have to all sleep on the ground. Even if they sleep on a foam rubber mattress or woven mat, it must be put on the floor.

During this Kanwariya festival, the entire government machinery in Deoghar stops functioning. The whole place caters to the Kanwariyas who are regarded as the guests of

Shiva. Mass arrangements are made by the local government, resting places are erected and home-guards posted en route to provide the necessary assistance. They see to their food, shelter, provisions, vegetables, snacks and so forth. Medical relief is also provided. Arrangements are also made along the way so that the pilgrims' water pots can be secured on special hangers at times of bathing and sleeping. All the government officers must attend to the lakhs of devotees who arrive every day on foot from Sultanganj; and the entire machinery, police, army and civil servants of the municipality are used to control the temple grounds. The number of pilgrims can reach two to three million, which is why there are so many hotels in Deoghar. At that time, you cannot get a labourer here to work. They all set up stalls along the way to sell tea, food and small emergency items. They make enough money for the whole year in one month.

No Kanwariya has returned disappointed or disillusioned in his staunch faith in Baba Baidyanath. It is believed that the wish of each and every person is fulfilled. Therefore, one must always be cautious when approaching this jyotirlinga, for in your ignorance you may ask for what is not really intended for you.

RIKHIA

Rikhia is a very beautiful place. I like this place so much that I have forgotten everything. I have left Munger and now I have settled down here and forgot myself, like a person who drinks too much and forgets his wife and children, and the entire world. It is five years since I came here, the sixth year will be completed this September. In order to settle down in a place, you need time. Now everything is favourable, the neighbourhood, the weather, the water, and my mind as well. This is my airport. My aircraft will fly away from here.

In this village, for miles and miles, there are no buildings, houses, offices or traffic jams. It is very peaceful. What you find here is just trees and fields, grazing cows and goats, cool breezes and pure air.

Silence or *mouna* is a luxury in crowded cities. This is why Rikhia is ideal; there is silence, stillness and timelessness in the atmosphere because of the simple life that people live here. At night you can experience absolute silence, except for the sound of frogs and crickets and nocturnal animals. Have you heard them? The nights here are crisp, clear and calm, although sometimes around midnight you may hear the barking of dogs, which is common in villages. Not only the Alakh Bara, but also the entire area becomes quiet by 6 or 7 pm and everyone is asleep by eight o'clock.

The carol you sing for the birth of Christ is, "Silent night, holy night; all is calm, all is bright." That must have been written with Rikhia in mind! For me, this is *ananda*, bliss. So, when I meditate, I do not have to encounter the useless chatter of either thought waves or sound waves, which can be a big hindrance in sadhana. In meditation, the mind becomes very sensitive and picks up all frequencies. Of course, I do not face any difficulty in meditation, even if it is the noisiest place, because I know how to block thoughts and sounds. This is also the reason why everybody likes mountains. Mountains supply energy, as they are created by energy explosions.

I have seen many beautiful places in the world, Kailash-Mansarovar, and so on, but I like this place very much. The people here are very simple and innocent, but I cannot say whether this will be lost in the future. I like the atmosphere, aura and magnetic force that radiates from within the people who live here. They are the energizing agents of the electromagnetic circuits or energy circuits in the body. The energy circuits in the body recharge from the environment and atmosphere, the air, trees and animals, from the creatures God or Nature has created, perhaps to give more energy and sustain the electromagnetic field pervading within and around us. You have to maintain a proper system to ensure that the electromagnetic circuit in the body has the right voltage. Where does this energy come from? It comes from a simple diet and pure atmosphere.

Yes, the ideal place to meditate is a place like Rikhia, where the air and water are pure, where the electromagnetic energy field is intact and thought frequencies are low. Do you know that the thoughts you think are released by you and travel as thought waves, and others pick them up knowingly or unknowingly? This is happening all the time in big cities where millions of people live and emit thought waves twenty-four-seven. Apart from thought waves, there is also an abundance of sound waves clashing with each other due to the constant chatter that people cannot live without. These chaotic waves enter our antahkarana and create physical and mental disturbances of one sort or another.

Another great thing is that every building you see in the Alakh Bara has been constructed by the local people who reside within a two-kilometre radius. The locals have done all the electricity, carpentry, civil engineering, preparation of land and planting of trees. We have not called anybody from outside, not even Deoghar. Of course, they are being paid for their good work. We have people with the knowhow, who can construct anything. They have made the kutir where I live. It is constructed entirely out of mud with a thatched roof, an environment-friendly house.

The Santhali people living here come to the Akhara every year on certain occasions to perform their tribal dances. They have made a bow and arrow for me, the same that they themselves use for hunting birds and small animals. The Santhalis are the original inhabitants of this land. The government law is that you cannot purchase this land from them. India is a free country, so generally you can purchase property anywhere, but here you cannot. It is very hard to get land in this area. All the plots of land have certain legal boundaries and there are many restrictions on transfer. These people here are very simple and nice; you could easily cheat them. When Europeans went to New York, they were very shrewd and purchased it for twenty-five dollars! You could do the same here. So, there are strict laws in this area, as in Kashmir. Here, if you can find unused land, you can build on it and make a home, but if you want to purchase a lot of land, it is not possible.

History of Rikhia

The name of this place is Rikhia and the name of my village is Paniya Pagar. Actually, the name 'Rikhia' comes from the word 'rishi', a place of sages and seers. This place has a very interesting history. Sri Aurobindo mentioned the name Rikhia in his autobiography. Sri Aurobindo's father and mother lived in a town near Deoghar. Before leaving for Pondicherry he came here to meet his wife. The *mukhia*, or chief, of Rikhia was here at that time and he remembers the visit. However, Sri Aurobindo lost the opportunity of having an ashram here because he was being chased by the British police. Otherwise, he would have stayed here because Pondicherry is by no means a place of pilgrimage. It is not an ancient place or a religious place, but he went there because it was a French pocket where he could hide from the British police and live peacefully.

A few years ago, another mahatma from Bengal, Sholmari Baba, came here. You may have read of him in the newspapers; he was thought to be Subhash Chandra Bose in disguise. There were several newspaper reports about him. He stayed here one full year. The family that lived on this property used to attend to these people, so this land has a spiritual samskara.

This property was very big initially. The Tagore family had considered the possibility of starting Shantiniketan here, but it did not work out. At one time somebody wanted to start a stone crushing industry here. The people of this area opposed it vehemently and got a stay order. Ultimately the plan was dropped. Now the government has passed an order that no industry can be started within a few kilometres of this place.

Let me remain here

Now, I do not have any personal thought of leaving this place. Of course, I keep myself open, not to your request, but to the commands which I receive. If I receive a phone call from Him, well, I have no choice, but even then I'll say, "God, please let me remain here." Our home is the abode of God. Of course, wherever I have lived has been full of blessings; every place has been auspicious for me. That is proof of God's benign hand. I remember four places. The first is my ancestral home where I was born and brought up, the second is my guru's ashram in Rishikesh, the third is the Bihar School of Yoga in Munger and the fourth is this Alakh Bara in Rikhia. All four places have been auspicious, full of grace and revelation.

In each of these places I received some spiritual experience. This is due to the grace of God; it has nothing to do with my luck, fate or fortune. Life is a combination of laughter and sorrow, birth and death. This world is not our permanent abode. This is not the real home of the *jivatma*, the individual soul. After completing my visit in this foreign land, I have to return to my original home. This is applicable to one and all. However, when God showers his grace, each and every place becomes auspicious.

For me the Lord of the whole world is here itself. The place where I am sitting is my temple. Wherever I am, I am within God's temple, and wherever I go, I go as a temple of God. He resides in me, but unfortunately I cannot see Him, because I am only a temple. In this temple, there should be a *pujari*, priest, who will worship and see God. What is the difference? This year I have decided that we will have the name of God chanted here so that it reverberates everywhere. People from all over the world will come here to sing the name of God. Blessed is Rikhia.

HARLA JORI TEMPLE

The first time I came to this temple was not to offer my worship. I just came here one morning because it is the nearest place for me to walk to, but I was wonderstruck when I felt the magnetic aura of this temple environment. Every place has energy, negative energy and positive energy. It is very powerful and I could not resist coming here. Every day in the early morning, I have been taking a trip here from the

Akhara, walking all alone, seeing the villagers on the road, and then I just sit down alone here. I am quite at home in Rikhia.

TRIKUT MOUNTAIN

They say this year there is a very good harvest and from the top of our Tribhuvan building, you can see all around for miles and miles. It is a beautiful scene. It is verdant all around the Alakh Bara. East of here is a very beautiful ancient mountain called Trikut. The word *trikut*, or *trikuti*, is synonymous with ajna chakra. Trikut Mountain is a lovely place. Next year when you come, be prepared to do some trekking up there. There are many caves, tigers, pythons and other snakes on that mountain.

3

My Neighbours

The villagers of Rikhia are very good people and they have accepted me with love. In fact, we are like one family. I get my bhiksha from them. They bring chappatis and vegetables for me. Whenever they do Kali pooja, they bring prasad for Bholenath. Right now, they are engaged in harvesting paddy. Out of the paddy, they will make flat rice and offer it at the Deoghar temple. It is an age-old tradition to offer it there, but since I have come here, they first offer it to me. So, by the end of this month, I will have quintals and quintals of flat rice.

The rural community in Rikhia is very poor, but they are humble people and live a life perfectly in balance with nature. They do not disturb nature for their own purpose, sustenance, greed or sensuality. They do not exploit nature, but live with nature. Any community that lives with nature follows a divine path. Nature is not created by divinity, but is a part of divinity. There is silence and simplicity in the lives of those who live with nature.

The poverty that these villagers live in is not self-imposed; it is a result of their situation. Nevertheless, it is a positive thing. Poverty is not a negative thing. It may be a negative thing for the greedy, the exploiters, the cheats and dacoits, but for those who are seeking spiritual life, poverty is not a negative state. In fact, if you want to experience spirituality, live like a poor person even if you are not poor. Reduce your wants, limit your needs and restrict your temptations. This does not go against the tenets of any religion; rather, this is what every religion has been saying for several millennia. There is no end to human desires. Desires will continue to grow. A restriction, limit or brake has to be put on them.

"Blessed are the meek, for they shall inherit the earth" – this is stated in the Bible. Blessed are the meek, the poor and the humble, because they shall inherit the earth. Poor people cannot assume arrogance. If they act arrogantly, they will be kicked by the rich. The poor do not have a chance. The only way for them is to be meek. The poor people have no profile in society. The meek and the humble people have no profile in our society. It is the wealthy, the affluent and the powerful that hold a high profile. These meek village people belong to the 'no profile' category. They have neither low profile nor high profile; they simply exist without any profile.

What do the women of this area do early in the morning? During autumn when the trees lose their leaves, they stir from their homes early and gather the fallen dry leaves. Sweeping them up with their brooms, they make a bundle of their collection, carry them on their heads and then store them in their houses. They don't go to the market to purchase firewood or gas cylinders. Some of you may not be aware of how independent they are. They use these dry leaves as firewood and cook their daily food in a small cooking pot. They don't need much.

It makes no difference to them whether there is a government or not. The dry leaves, the cooking pot, the fire, and one's stomach, are all there. No social or governmental intervention is required. This is an independent culture. They draw water for cooking and drinking purposes from the village tank. They go to the fields to relieve themselves and their ablutions are finished by sunrise. Thus they lead a spartan life independent of external aids.

    This kind of culture is not dependent on a king, on wealth or on any other resources. It depends on no external resources. If there is no government or king, they can survive on their own. When I meet the village people, I often say, "With a pushcart you are independent. You earn sixty rupees a day and live an honest life. You need not earn six hundred rupees a day and be dishonest!"

    Yes, the Bible proclaims that these are the people who will inherit this earth, for they will continue to exist for millions and millions of years. They are so simple and meek that they can survive in any condition and not raise a voice. They have survived amidst the ravages of nature, they have survived without a roof over their head, they have survived the pangs of hunger, and they have survived the dangers of living with snakes, scorpions and mosquitoes. You would not survive even one day on the water they drink or the food they eat! This is why they will inherit the earth.

The affluent who live in comfort cannot survive in calamities. These meek and humble village people will outlive all calamities and start afresh. If they do not survive, your earth will become barren, because you are not strong enough to inherit the earth. This is what I have read in the Bible, this is what I have read in the Koran, this is what I have read in the Upanishads, and this is what I have seen in these poor village people of Rikhia.

Village lifestyle

There are villagers all around me in this area, and they are very simple at heart. They are also very poor. They like me very much, because they find that I am even poorer than them. I have settled here in the village. I am inherently a man of village. This is a great solace to them, because they at least have one dhoti, but I do not even have that. I can live with them in much the same way as they live themselves. However, if I were to live with them like a rich man, then they would be jealous of me.

The conditions in which the people of this country have survived, nobody else could have survived. Go and look in the villages. See how they live all together in small rooms! They have a lot of stamina, strong immune systems, immunity to disease. See the dirty water they drink, and still they manage. Village people should never think that poverty is a curse. Poverty is not a curse, nor is affluence a boon. You simply have to change your way of thinking regarding this issue.

People come to meet me and they bring blankets, clothes, children's toys, books and many other things. We distribute them to the villagers who live around here. They then have at least a warm blanket to ward off the cold. That is the only interaction that interests me; the rest does not mean anything. Rikhia is my airport and my aircraft will fly away from here. I have not come here from my own desire; I was asked to come. The villagers have accepted me with love.

There was a boy of twelve years who could not walk straight. When I asked, "What's the matter?" his parents said that the boy could not see because he was going blind. I found out that the boy had cataract and his parents did not know about it, because they did not have the means to go to a doctor, even in Deoghar town, ten kilometres away. This disease is curable. We sent him to a doctor who implanted a lens in his eye, and now the boy can see. Wherever there are severe limitations, that is poverty.

Dharma is no longer the foundation of the nation. In today's context, the nation is the foundation for dharma. What is then the foundation of the nation? It is the *samskriti*, or the culture, which you see among the poor people here. Some of you may not have lived in a village, and to you my advice is to live in one for some time to experience that life and see the skills that they use for survival, the survival of the fittest.

Definition of 'neighbour'

Ayam nijah paroveti gananaa laghuchetasaam,
Udaaracharitaanaam tu vasudhaiva kutumbakam.

For those with an open heart the whole world becomes their neighbourhood.

In 1991, on the day of *Kartika Poornima*, when the moon is brightest, God gave me a very good idea. He told me, "Help your neighbours as I have helped you." Then I had to consider, what does the word 'neighbour' mean? Is it the person who lives next door or close to my house? For a man whose heart is open, the whole world is his neighbourhood and everyone is his neighbour. One who has a small, closed heart thinks in terms of, 'This is mine and that is yours.' He makes a division between what is mine and what is yours, but I do not want to be limited by that thought. Rather, I believe that everything belongs to You, O God, because You have given it to me. You are the owner, the giver, the treasurer. You are the ocean of prosperity, grace, mercy and love. You gave everything to me so that I could give it to others.

Who is my neighbour? When God showers His grace upon me the whole world will become my neighbourhood.

When this happens I will say, "My daughter sitting in London has a boil on her head. Send her medicine from this or that doctor." Then there will be a thought for everybody, everywhere. For God, the whole world is like a neighbourhood. God has a thought for everybody. He takes care of all people. He has asked Maya, who is also Prakriti and Devi, to look after His children. The father is not home, so the mother runs the household and looks after the children. The whole show is run by Devi, that's what I've heard. But just now Rikhia is my immediate neighbourhood. Paniya Pagar is my village; Amarwa is my immediate neighbour; and Rikhia is my very close neighbour. Ten lakh bighas, twenty lakh bighas, this is a neighbourhood.

What is the definition of a neighbour? 'Neighbouring' means nearby, next to you. Nowadays, what does 'neighbouring' mean? During ancient days, 'neighbouring' used to mean next to my house. These days, the whole world is next door; the whole world is a neighbourhood, especially when you can leave Delhi in the morning at four o'clock and reach London in the evening! In four or six hours you can go from one corner of the world to the other. So all people are your kith and kin and now many of your relations need your help in the form of selfless service. I am speaking to everybody.

Work which you do free of charge is called *nishkama seva*, selfless work, action without desire for fruit. Why is selfless service necessary? It is necessary for self-transformation. It is necessary to clean the rajoguna and tamoguna of the mind. Nishkama seva is like detergent. Nishkama seva does not only mean work; rather, it means that you should have a feeling for it in your heart. This is what I learned in my guru's ashram when I was working for him. It is not a question of performing pious acts, but it is necessary to attune oneself to God. One has to think along these lines.

You may practise mantra or prayers, you may go to a temple or church, but never forget your neighbour, the unfortunate person who is suffering, who does not have what he needs. What he does not have, you and I have in plenty. If I have ten loaves of bread, I can easily give away five because he needs them and I do not. This good sense came to me only after coming to Rikhia.

Reach out to people
If you visit forty odd houses in rural India you will come across scarcity, dearth, suffering, poverty, darkness and dejection. There is nothing else. As an exception you may come across a house where it is different, but for millions and millions of people the state of affairs is abysmal. They have no shelter, no food, no place to cook, no toilet, not even water to drink.

What have you done for such people? You are wasting your time if you just grapple and wrestle with your own mind twenty-four hours a day. Nobody thinks of going to the house of a poor man and lighting a lamp. Nobody thinks of visiting the have-nots. If a child is born in a poor family, at least go and give the child a crib. When a child is to be born in your own family you immediately think of a crib and there are elaborate preparations in anticipation. When there is a newborn in someone else's family, however, all you do is give good wishes and greetings. If you only give good wishes and greetings to the poor man, that will not help him. Go to his house and give him a warm sweater, some tonic for the mother and some money.

This is a practical sadhana I am giving you. I do it and Swami Satsangi does it. One day she went out and Ramu, a village mason who works here, was making his way home. He called her and said, "See, I have children." His wife had given birth to twins. Swami Satsangi came and informed me. She said, "He is asking for a name for his twins. What names would you suggest for them?" I said to her, "Forget about naming them. First give them a crib, give medicine, get a doctor, and cut the umbilical cord. Take Swami Suryabindu to treat the wound with antiseptic. A name you can give tomorrow or even in nine days. What is the urgency?" If you want to befriend your mind, listen to me. Treat the whole world as your family and reach out to as many people as you can.

If you feed the hungry or help a poor person, that is *sat karma*, selfless or divine karma. Sat karma is any act you do that helps somebody physically, mentally, spiritually, monetarily or in any other way. That is the teaching which is coming up now through me. I have not made any changes in my thinking. My guru, Swami Sivananda, always emphasized that service is the stepping stone to spiritual life. He used to say, "Serve, love and give." So I have not made any change in the teachings, and what shape they will take in the future I do not know. Now the plight of widows has come into the focus of my mind. From next year, 1998, we will be helping the widows of this area. Whatever I have, whatever I can manage, I will consecrate to them during my lifetime and even after that. This is a trial project that will improve the area. In the course of time I can see very clearly that thousands of young, brilliant, fresh, enthusiastic, energetic boys and girls will take up this work throughout the rural sectors of India. They will go to each village and live and work with the village people for their upliftment.

It is very important to protect the natural culture of this country. I can clearly see a new type of sannyasin, who will be free from selfishness and personal ambitions, whose main thought will be how to help others. Helping others is praying to God; living amongst the poor and needy is living with God. Your family and children are spread all over the world. They are all your brothers and sisters. Try to enlarge the scope of your family and get out of that little cage of husband, wife and children – "We two and our two". Why not say, "Husband, wife, children and other children?" That is *atmabhava*, feeling yourself in others, and by developing this feeling, the possibility of enlightenment becomes greater.

Lend a helping hand
Christ and the saints have all said, "Love thy neighbour," because to love is very difficult. It is difficult because you don't know how to love; you don't know the ABC of love. What is love? "You are mine, I am yours?" No, that is not it. You don't know what love is. Love is an art and a science that you will have to learn. Love is not being emotional and passionate. Saying, "I love you, I love you" to your beloved does not necessarily mean that you really love him or her. Love is an expression of purity that manifests when you become very strong within your own heart. That is why the saints have always emphasized love. You prepare yourself for love by small acts of kindness. There has to be some elementary training in love. The elementary training, the ABC of love is little acts of kindness.

What are little acts of kindness? Swami Sivananda said, "Be good, do good, be kind, be compassionate." Once he completely cleaned out the whole ashram. We had no blankets because he had given them all away. The first thing he used to say was, "Namo Narayan, are you all right?" Swami Sivananda always used to think about others. Whenever he met people, he did not give spiritual lessons such as I give. He always used to say nice things about people and he would give them clothes or food and medicine for their sickness and disease. He could remember the names of each one of his acquaintances from thirty-five to forty years ago. If a man had become old, he would then ask, "How is your grandson? He was in the eighth class. Where is he now? What he is doing? He had a mole here. Is the mole still there?" You should know about the man whom you love. If I love you, I should know everything about you, especially your difficulties, problems, ambitions and desires. If I know nothing about you, if I do not want to know anything about you, then I cannot care for you.

Therefore, love is a very difficult thing. The philosophy of love and bhakti should be well understood. When mankind learns how to love and serve one another, to be kind and tolerant of one another, to help one another and to share the problems, worries and ideas of others, then your family, your society and the world will be a better place to live in.

Helping is my passion
Now I am seventy-five and I have been working in spiritual life since the age of eighteen. I started my spiritual career with tantric practices, then spent twelve years with my guru, nine years as a vagabond, and twenty years at Bihar School of Yoga. During all those years the only inner enlightenment I received was what I read in books. Now I am here in Rikhia and I am always thinking, "How can I help this family? How can I help that man? How can I help that little girl who is suffering from polio or arthritis?" These ideas come to me all the time, even in dreams.

Here in Rikhia, I am very attached to the people of the local area. I always talk about that man's daughter who is going to get married, that man's wife who is sick, that tuberculosis patient who did not come for his medicine the last time. I am attached to them and they are attached to me, but does this attachment bind me? Is this attachment bondage? Is this attachment an outcome of my ignorance? Will it corrupt my soul? Will it make me unhappy? Will it make me wretched? No. When you love others who do not come in the category of 'mine', when you have attachment to people who are not yours, who are outside the category of 'we two and our two', at that time, attachment is a very positive and constructive quality. A person without proper attachment is worthless, just like an unripe vegetable.

Only last night I was dreaming of a lady in a nearby village whose husband is very sick. I gave him a cycle rickshaw, but he cannot ride it now. She is young, maybe thirty-five, and has two children. So, I was thinking of how to help her, because you cannot help people by just giving money. In the dream, I saw that she was approaching an officer and so I knew she would somehow get a job in a government department, earning maybe two thousand rupees a month, which would be enough for her family to live on.

Now, do you call such thoughts worldly or spiritual? I was thinking of that girl yesterday and talking to somebody about how to find her a job so that she can have regular earnings and feed her children. I am not talking about yoga now; I am talking about bread and butter. How will she get it? We built a house for her last year. I called Surya, a mason from Italy, along with some other swamis, and they built her a house nearby. I am looking after her welfare, but I do not give her money. I will see that she gets some work, or a shop, so that she can be independent. The ideas that often come to my mind now about helping others never used to come before, because I was very selfish. I always thought about God and samadhi: savikalpa samadhi, nirvikalpa samadhi, ritambhara prajna, cosmic experience. All those things came to my mind, but now helping my neighbours has become my obsession, my passion.

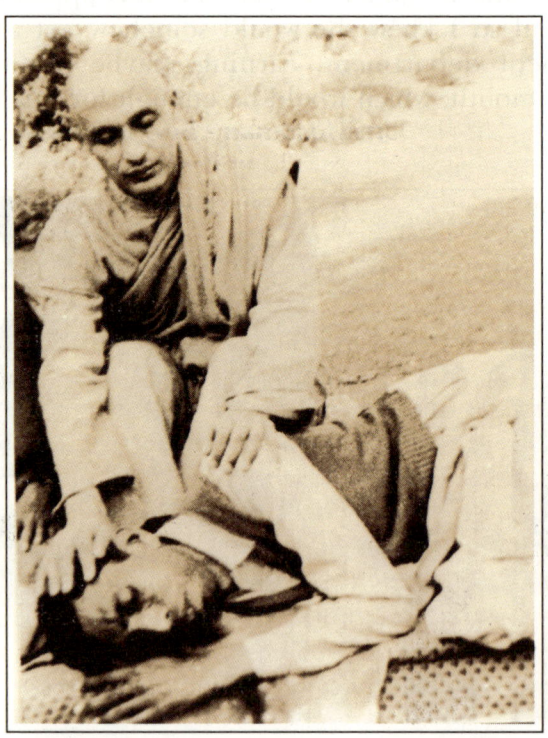

When God sends inspiration

In Rishikesh, I had ample scope and opportunities for *seva*, service. Swami Sivananda's fundamental philosophy of life was social service, human service. He used to place *Bhagavat bhajan*, singing God's name, at the bottom of the priority list. His priorities were "Serve, love, give, purify, meditate, realize." So, meditation was at the end of his list, a long way off. Whereas you start your spiritual life with meditation, my guru's spiritual life started with service and culminated in meditation.

Swami Sivananda used to call in the sweepers and scavengers, wash their feet and feed them. My response to that was negative. I found it useless and irrelevant for spiritual evolution. However, being his disciple, I did render service. I cleaned, cooked and fed the scavengers, but my heart was not in it. There were many lepers in Rishikesh lined up along the roads and pathways. Once, Swamiji thought of settling them in proper housing. He was given some land by Tehri Maharaj where some houses were built for the lepers. He gave each one a goat and also bundles of bidis, and told them not to go begging in the streets.

I was given the duty of going amidst the lepers and the sick to read and teach them the *Ramacharitamanas* and *Ramayana*, but my heart was not in the work. I used to accompany the doctors and distribute drugs and medicines among the lepers. I performed all the duties, but not from my heart. However, when God inspires you to do service, you take it as His blessing. The work and service that are being carried out here in Rikhia are not discharged as social service, but in compliance with God's will, in obedience to His command. This is the fulfilment of His wish; He tells me what to do and I obey. Now, not only my heart but also my whole being is given in service to my neighbours.

Atmabhava

Atmabhava means feeling for others like you do for yourself. When your son falls sick, what happens to you? Yet, when someone else's son falls sick in your neighbourhood, you just say, "Give him cortisone." That's all. You do not think beyond that. Nothing happens in the heart. Nothing happens in the head either. You go to sleep peacefully although his son is still sick. You have done your work, applied this medicine and called that doctor. You can make the phone calls, you may even take him to the doctor by ambulance, but the feeling that you have when your child is sick doesn't come for someone else's son, because there is no atmabhava there. If we do not expand the atmabhava, the sense of selfhood, then all sadhana is useless. Do not live only for those who belong to you. Live a little for others also. You cannot totally share the happiness and sorrows of the world, as that is only possible for God, but in some little way share the sorrows of others. You have to find a place in your heart for people who are not known to you. You have to act out your compassion and feelings on behalf of these people. Consolation with words only is not enough.

To think on behalf of others in the same way that we think about ourselves is the true test of Vedanta. To think, 'I am Brahman, you are Brahman' does not work. You can say it, but there is nothing in it. Atmabhava means feeling for others in the same way that you feel for yourself. It is written in the first Upanishad itself, the *Ishavasya Upanishad*: "Let your suffering be my suffering, my suffering be your suffering."

Good samskaras

I don't see these people very often. The best way for a sannyasin to contact the masses is not to meet them. He should remain in seclusion, do his sadhana, chant the Lord's name and do pooja. For a few days in a year, he may meet the people and tell them whatever has to be told. There is no need to go to each house like a social worker and spend hours talking to them; that does not work. A dog's tail cannot be straightened that easily.

'Backward class' means deprived in monetary terms, education, assets, but not in samskaras. These people have good samskaras. They are not backward in samskaras. It is possible that Indian culture is alive only due to them. However educated and powerful a society may be, unless the family structure is strong, the society disintegrates. Good samskaras must come before wealth, and they will come only when people work hard and struggle. A free supply of goods does not work. Education becomes unnecessary. Therefore, the samskaras are growing slowly here and the chiefs of the different villages understand these things.

Family system

A necklace, no matter how beautiful, be it of gold, diamond or pearl, will scatter unless there is a thread through it. Similarly, only if the family ties are strong can a family live in unity and harmony while preserving the best samskaras. This trait is present in all the backward classes. The family ties are very strong. They also sacrifice a lot for the family. For example, our driver could get a good job in Delhi paying five thousand rupees per month, but he will not leave his wife, children and parents for the money.

This is a very good samskara; he has sacrificed money for family unity. He may be earning only seven to eight hundred rupees per month here, whereas in Delhi, he could be employed in a good company. If he goes to Delhi, however, his family life will disintegrate: either he will live alone there, or take his wife and children, leaving his parents alone back here. I have tried sending a number of people outside for employment, but they have all refused. They say they will only work if I provide a job somewhere close by.

The people of backward classes are very conscious of their family system. For a strong national identity, a strong, well planned and well organized family structure is an absolute necessity. Once disintegration starts within the family structure, we will be faced with the same situation that is prevailing in every family in the European countries today. Within thirty to forty years, civilization will come to an end. Our destruction is very near indeed therefore we must give up our old prejudices.

Dharma, right conduct, asks us to care for our younger brothers who are weak, lame, blind or disabled. If one of our sons is a graduate or a postgraduate, a professor, doctor or lecturer, and the other son is disabled, will you take equal care of them? Which one will you serve more? Surely the disabled son. It is the social responsibility of each one of us and even the upper crust of backward castes, to provide an opportunity to those who are handicapped in income, resources and education.

Each and every person desires respect and status in life. If there is an illiterate woman from the village, do I have the right to shoo her away just because I am educated and she is not? No, she is one of us. We should treat her with as much respect as she desires and expects. In fact, more attention is due to this lady, because she is handicapped by her lack of education.

In the 1950s, when I went to Chennai, even a shopkeeper would shout at a shudra to go away, so that not so much as the air off the shudra's body was inhaled by him. Money, even currency notes, accepted from the shudra were washed in water. In Sitamarhi, I stayed in the house of a *kayastha* (a relatively higher caste) whose mother would wash firewood, possibly chopped by a shudra, before using it. She would even wash the clothes brought in by the dhobi. I once asked her, "Do you also wash the sugar?"

We have all defaulted. The entire population from the Himalayas to Kanyakumari is guilty of this idiocy. Our country has had leaders of stature, belonging to various castes, who ruled over the hearts of the masses. However, should a thakur, brahmin or kayastha fall in love and marry a girl from a different caste, there is mass furore. What is so extraordinary about this? It is a marriage between a man and a woman, not between a man and a horse!

Amongst the four castes, the brahmins used to rule, but as soon as the kshatriyas took up the sword, they grabbed their rights. The brahmins, however, were clever and said, "All right, you can be the king and we will be

the prime ministers", knowing that the real power lies with the prime minister. Then came the vaishyas with financial powers. Again the brahmins said, "Fine, you be the financial advisers", and included them in the fold. The remaining population became the working class, whom we call *shramjeevi,* and they are the majority. All revolutions the world over, have been initiated by them. The working classes of India, like the rest of its population, are basically simple people. Their nature has been tempered through the reading of the *Bhagavad Gita* and *Ramayana.*

To prevent our working classes from becoming destructive, it is imperative that our principles, our laws, should be in accordance with justice. If the majority of the population of this nation remain hungry and ill-clad, there will be a rise in crime and other social disturbances, and you will be the cause of it. The prosperous will be insecure. Their daughters may be kidnapped and sold in the metropolitan cities for paltry sums of money. This should not happen.

The distinction between dharma and adharma must be made. What is dharma? The *shastras*, scriptures, have specified that the first definition of dharma is *paropakara,* doing good towards others. There is no religion higher than service to humanity, and no sin greater than causing harm to others. While living with your parents, children, friends or neighbours, if you are constantly aware of their needs and working for their welfare, it is called paropakara. It has many names. This is dharma. Causing pain and suffering to others is adharma. This is the definition.

Relationship with the local people

All of these people sitting here in front of me are connected with this institution in one way or another. They are from the nearby villages of Paniya Pagar, Lodhia, Amavar, Nawadih, Devichak, Pairhidih and Rudrapur. I have to throw some light on these villagers. When I came to Rikhia in 1989 there was nothing in this area, it was a desolate place. People living in my neighbourhood were living like orphans and had no hope for the future. I have completed twelve years of my stay here and during this period the conditions of the people in this *panchayat*, our village council, have improved remarkably.

My arrival has made a substantial change to their destiny. You might all have witnessed that change. Many activities are taking place, such as education. The boys and girls all go to school. There is almost one hundred percent education among the children. Every one of them now goes to school. Girls have been provided with bicycles so they can travel independently and safely to Deoghar for higher education. The level of education has become very high here and the chosen language of this area is English. These girls are not the children of office workers; they come from the families of labourers, rickshaw pullers, coolies, ploughmen, transplanters, weavers and tailors.

After I came to Rikhia, the electricity supply became constant. I compelled the electricity department to install transformers so they now receive electricity. Prior to that, although electrical wires had been put up from Deoghar to Rikhia, there was never any power. Last evening, after the electricity went off, a phone call was made directly to the chairman of BSEB (Bihar State Electricity Board). The call was not made to the electrical engineer but straight to the chairman to ask him to resume the supply. We have established a relationship with these rural people.

I often go for a stroll to these villages, sometimes one way and sometimes the other way. People watch out for me and the children say 'good morning' to me. If somehow they miss seeing me, then the children start shouting at their parents, "Mummy, Papa, Swamiji has gone past." Some of these villagers were not born when I came here in 1989. The twelve-year-old boys and girls have no knowledge of my arrival. It is not because I give them anything. As a matter of fact, love is quite reciprocal. When you love someone you receive the same amount of love in return. If I ignore you, then you are bound to ignore me too. When you extend your hand in friendship I become your friend. When you wish to be my companion I follow suit. This means either you have compelled me or I have compelled you. We have compelled each other. Friendship or comradeship is a great victory. Friendship is the most powerful weapon of mankind. The promotion of friendliness is great politics. Are you listening? The attainment of friendship is great politics.

Load bearers of society
The people living here, within a radius of three to four kilometres of the Akhara, are all skilled labourers: motor mechanics, electricians, masons, gardeners. In a way, I have become attached to them; my bhavana has found a harmony with them. There is nothing superficial about them in behaviour or in dress. They do not take any synthetic food or wear synthetic clothes, nor do they have synthetic love. Everything about them is natural. If I did not get food from the ashram, these villagers would provide

it. They send food for me and also for my dog Bholenath. Whenever there is a festival or pooja, they send his share. But they are very poor. I have seen poverty before, but never so close.

These villagers are very simple and very poor people, yet they are the load bearers of our society. They are very mobile people, very strong people. They are the weight bearers of our society. Do you know what load bearers are? Just as beams and columns bear the load of a building, similarly, the common folk in any country, the labourers, taxi drivers, rickshaw pullers and thela pullers, are the load bearers of society.

If this section of society cracks and breaks, then there will be chaos. People like us are the interior decoration. We are the load; we are not the load-bearers. They are the load bearers of our society and once they crack, society will break. Therefore, it is very important that we recognize their role in society and also accept their existence as a reality. It is our duty in every society, eastern or western, African, Chinese or Russian, to care for the common folk, because their needs are very few. What they consume in one year, an American or European consumes in one second. I am talking about their consumption of oxygen, food and water. Can you understand how economical they are for your existence, for your society? We have to learn this lesson.

So, I am very glad that the villagers will receive prasad. They have been receiving prasad since I came here, but this time I wanted to tell all of you that you have a duty, a compulsory obligation. In every society, not only in India, there are common people who tend cows, take care of sheep, drive taxis and do all kinds of other jobs like plumbing and electricity. They are the supports of your society. When society breaks, anarchy takes place. Anarchy does not take place because there is a lot wrong with us. If we are destroyed, nothing will happen. But if their society is destroyed the country will go to the dogs. It has always happened in history and that is why we Indians are very careful about it. Everywhere in India they are invited to yajnas.

I want to emphasize the point that the general populace are the load bearers of society and the foundation of the nation. The king is not the cornerstone of the country or the nation. It is the subjects, the masses that provide the base, the solid ground, the direction, the destination for a nation to move forward; not the king or the ruler. The king cannot build the nation; it is the masses who build the nation. The ruler is just our representative. He cannot be our master. The rulers are our servants. The subjects are above the king. Intellectuals and their ideologies are numbered. Newspapers and magazines highlight their activities and it appears that they constitute the core of society, but they do not represent the philosophy of the masses.

That sixty to seventy percent of the population will determine the national philosophy of India. The cultivators, the labourers, the downtrodden and the destitute constitute the mass of the Indian population and they will determine the philosophy.

Recognizing local talent

We utilize the services of the villagers for brick making, carpentry, housing construction, welding. Everything is done here locally – my neighbours have done a lot to improve this area. I did not hire any artisans or mechanics from Kanpur, Kolkata, Delhi or Mumbai. We do not hire people from Deoghar or any other town now. There has been no contract work. We have engaged local labourers. If our water pump is out of order, then the mechanic comes from a nearby village to repair it. The painting, whitewashing, electrical works, every item of work is taken care of by local artisans.

My neighbours have done everything: digging excavations, installing pipes, erecting canopies. They have done the bricklaying, electrical fittings and plumbing and set up the transformers you see on the premises. They have installed all the structures you see here: the canopies, the pandals and the pavilion. They have also set up the sewage system, and you will not find such an efficient system even in Delhi! Now this area is humming with life. Activities are going on around the clock.

Some of these villagers are cultivators; others are labourers, push carters, rickshaw pullers and porters. Quite a few own tempos and trekkers, which are their means of livelihood. Some are 'toddy tappers', they take out juice from the toddy trees. A number of people drink toddy. The world cannot be free of toddy takers. God has created a strange world which consists of many types of people. He has created many obstructions too, on the way to moksha. He probably thought that if all living beings became liberated, then who would worship God? People remember God and recount His virtues only when they are in distress, and when they are out of the woods they forget God. So God devised a plan to put people in distress and misery so that they may remember

Him and recount His virtues. When there is no pain and distress, then what is the role of God? I have just told you all this by way of a joke. I don't know how far it is from the truth. It is up to you to judge what the truth is.

These village people have received a lot of inspiration, help and encouragement. More than anything else, they have received an identity. 'Rikhia', the name of their village, is now on the world map.

Equal pay

We do not discriminate between male and female workers here. In the past, the daily rate was eighteen rupees for men and sixteen rupees for women. When I asked why the rate was lower for women, I was told it was the practice prevalent in this area. I said, "Let the practice go to the dogs. Women work harder than men and their output is greater than men's. So why should we pay women less?" Thereafter men and women have been paid equally in this ashram. I do not discriminate. At that time I used to pay them eighteen rupees. Now the daily wage has gone up to sixty rupees.

Here is Fakku, my oldest disciple in Rikhia. When I first came here she was a small child. Now she has grown up and married. If I need anything, I just contact her and she gets it for me. She is Swami Satsangi's best friend.

Namo Narayan

It is always said that Rama's name should be repeated in Deoghar and *Om Namah Shivaya* in Ayodhya. In Ayodhya repeat Shiva's name and Rama will be pleased; in Deoghar repeat Rama's name and Shiva will be pleased.

When I came to Rikhia the villagers greeted me by saying, "Pranam, Swamiji." I said to them, "*Namo Narayan*." Today, all the children of our panchayat chant only one mantra: *Namo Narayan*. In the whole of their lives they have never uttered *Om Namah Shivaya*. That shows how simple and innocent these people are. They are a very unlucky lot. Society, the elders, the government have all betrayed them, but their children say, "*Namo Narayan*." When passing this way while walking along the road, they say, "*Namo Narayan*."

4

Village Development

Whoever comes to Rikhia must come with the intention of helping others. They can provide help physically, and if they are physically incapable, they can help in other ways.

In Bihar, the public welfare activities and plans for development have not been extended to the villages at all. All the development has been restricted to big cities like Patna, Jamshedpur and Ranchi. Those cities have good buildings, schools, colleges, hospitals and nursing homes. Good roads, bridges, parks and hotels are constructed there, but the villages have nothing. The politicians have not forced the government to reach out to the villages. Reaching out to the villages means that no one in a village dies hungry and that when their cows come on heat they have the facilities nearby for quick insemination and do not have to walk for ten or twelve kilometres, dragging the cow along behind them.

Another neglected aspect is primary health care. I am not talking about serious diseases like tuberculosis, just routine diseases. The villagers do not have proper drinking water; they get jaundice from infected water. The women and children of the villages have not yet understood that education is for their benefit. In other states like Haryana, Maharashtra, Andhra Pradesh and Tamil Nadu, the rays of progress and development have touched each and every village. The sun of progressive modern culture has illuminated them. Adequate facilities to live a decent life have reached the villages in these states.

The farmers of Haryana are much better off than here, because the basic commodities of water, seeds and fertilizer have been provided there and they have also been given moral encouragement. Farmers are a struggling community, as five acres of land requires the same infrastructure as fifteen, whether it is an irrigation pump, a tractor, or a plough and bullocks. However, the villagers here do not have these things. So what do they do? One farmer has a bull and another farmer also has a bull, so they join the two together and plough their land in turn. By the time people pair up the oxen and plough each other's fields by turns, the position of the planets has changed and it is no longer auspicious to sow seeds.

Since arriving here, I have started donating bullocks because farming cannot be done without them, just as your crops cannot be grown without seeds. Farmers who live in the villages are very poor and their biggest need is not land, but facilities. The government has given them land, but agriculture is not done by a land lease alone; water, seeds, a plough and bulls are needed.

Government support was given for the production of coal, steel and mica; the same support was not given to agriculture. A family cannot eat coal and steel. For building construction, you need cement and iron, for fuel you need coal, but the farmers, who are the backbone, the root and basis of our society and our country, have been deprived. I see this all around me and that is the reason why Bihar has remained backward. As long as the leaders ignore the basic needs of the poor villages, their leadership will remain fruitless for themselves as well as for society. It will have no positive or permanent consequences.

The real emancipation of India will happen only with the emancipation of the villages. The poverty is mainly in the villages and since all the public utilities are concentrated

in the cities, the village people are migrating there. In the cities there are schools and colleges, but the villages have nothing. If a villager is posted to Deoghar or Patna, he calls his family and children there and the village is left behind. All the people who are weak, crippled and otherwise devoid of quality are left behind. How can we bring back that dynamic quality? Educated, capable, prosperous people have originally come from the villages; they are the forceful community. Now, there is no strong community in the villages and no facilities or resources are available. What can be done to raise the standard of village living so that we can live there once again?

The needs of a local villager are basically those of a farmer. A labourer has no special needs; he can go from place to place. But how can a farmer leave his land and go away? Five bighas of land is enough to support a family if it is properly utilized. In Australia, the ashram had a farm of around five bighas and the swamis did the farming there.

They grew their own vegetables and had a cold storage facility. Every morning the swamis would harvest the vegetables and put them in cold storage. People came to the ashram to practise asana and pranayama and left carrying carrots and cauliflowers.

INDIA'S FUTURE LIES IN VILLAGES

The definition of India is nine hundred thousand villages; about seventy percent of the population live a village life. I came from a village and many among you might also have come from a village, even if you do not live there now. It is possible that two generations ago your ancestors migrated to a city, but essentially you belong to a village.

India is a nation of villages. India has always been an agricultural country. There used to be only seven cities here, the rest of the country was rural. This means that for most people in India, the means of living is agriculture-based, yet these people have been completely neglected in the last fifty years. Agriculture is related to villages, while market is related to cities. In such a situation it is essential that the government invests in villages. Right now, the distribution of money to villages is miniscule and agriculture and farming do not get a good foundation. That is the truth.

Since the ancient times, rural villages produce the most important thing, food. The world can run without computers, television, tables and silk, but no one can stay alive without food and water: the villages give you life. However, in the twenty-first century, the villages of India are handicapped and they have no facilities. A villager who owns five acres of land cannot provide for his children. To farm five acres of land you need infrastructure: electricity, pumps to provide water, and at least two bulls to plough the land. The government does not provide these basic facilities, so how will a villager earn? Where will he get money from? He could have these facilities if there was an industry close to the village where members of the family worked and contributed their earnings into farming. This option does not exist here.

Until the villages are uplifted, this country will not rise. A country cannot rise by ignoring one hundred million of its population. If the current trend continues, poverty and prosperity will both go up where they are. People in the cities have immense wealth, but that wealth does not get distributed. It is for this reason that backwardness, poverty, illiteracy, squalor and lawlessness have become rampant in India and have isolated the villages. Most of the government money is spent in the cities, therefore people from the villages rush to the cities and overcrowd them. Once a villager lives in the city he goes out of gear; he gets corrupted and goes astray. He gets culture shock; he wants to drink Pepsi and Coke instead of pure, fresh water.

If you go to the western countries, you will find that the governments employ huge funds in villages. In a village the size of Rikhia you will find two or three five-star hotels, swimming pools and banks. Until the government pays attention to villages, the problem of poverty will not be solved. Every nation must watch out for its 'spine'. If your spine becomes weak, your entire body becomes weak. The spine of India is its villages. The condition that we have in India today is because the government has completely ignored villages. This needs to be given serious thought.

Self-sufficiency
The problem with villages these days is that not everyone who lives in the village works there. Now, the young people go off to school so that they can become clerks and wear fancy shirts and trousers. The youth are then attracted in a different direction. To have earning power is one thing; self-sufficiency is another. Self-sufficiency is superior because you do not have to depend on anyone. All that is required are some vegetables from the garden, some milk from the cow which grazes on your land, and some grain that also grows on your land. One does not need anything else.

Once in a while, the man can work as a casual labourer and earn twenty to twenty-five rupees daily for other minor expenses. The family then lives in *ananda*, bliss. This is called self-sufficiency. Earning enables the family to buy their necessities such as vegetables, turmeric, spices, flour, pulses and rice from the market. In order to be able to buy all these items, the ability to earn is necessary. However, at present, to earn one has to live in the town or city, which means moving out of the village, paying rent, electricity bills and taxes. In this way, life within the society becomes complicated. In the next twenty or thirty years, all the cities of India will be filled to the brim and the villages will become empty. All able villagers will migrate to cities and they will visit their native villages only occasionally. However, there will come a time when they will return to the villages with money, for only the rich can live in villages. Then the old villages will all vanish.

Invest in rural facilities

What is the percentage of spending in villages? How do you expect that a villager will have money and facilities? The future of India lies in villages, not in cities. Not just of India, but for the whole world the future lies in villages. Human civilization grows in villages. Therefore, think about this and act so that seventy percent investment is made in rural areas.

In Western countries, a huge amount of money is generated in villages, just as in cities, but this does not happen in India. If money does not generate in the villages, why will the government invest there? It is normal logic. In the West, the urban and the wealthy people are encouraged to live in villages. In Australia, all who live in villages are wealthy, whereas here, all who live in villages are poor. They cannot even buy a pump to drill for water; they cannot feed a pair of bulls. Why is there no money here? Because money does not get generated here.

If India wants political, social and economic eminence in the competing global market it should give priority to its villages. In a global economy there is greater possibility of unemployment and concentration of capital. To prevent this we should bring the US, Swiss, German or French systems in the villages because the villages will continue to exist. No villager in India is ready to leave his village or land. That is a good thing, but the concentration of investment is not there. Therefore, we should go towards villages. The biggest gap between cities and villages is that those who live in the cities receive too many modern services and those in the villages receive none. They do not have any means of mass communication to learn the latest technology in farming, cattle keeping or poultry. They continue to follow the old methods and thus do not move out of their dire poverty.

Changing needs of society

Every society has separate needs. What the US needs, rural India does not need and what is needed in rural India, the US does not want. What is happening in Europe? The Christian religion is almost breathing its last. Why? European society does not require bread and butter; it does not need the hospitals that we need here. European

society needs spiritual leaders like Swami Vivekananda, Bhaktivedanta, Maharishi Mahesh Yogi and the like. They are required there. You have to quickly identify the requirements of a society. What is needed in Europe, in England, we do not need in village India. We need good schools and colleges, hospitals and gurukuls, development and investment in all village and rural facilities, and they need yoga, meditation, the Upanishads, the *Bhagavad Gita* and gurus. You can see this with your own eyes. Sannyasins will have to acquire that understanding. Swami Vivekananda understood that; he was a brilliant person. Maharishi Mahesh Yogi also understood that.

Modernization

For a large country like India, information technology is essential; it is a gateway to wealth. Communication and information can have a big market here. It is not practical to connect the different corners of such an enormous country with cables. It has to be connected through satellites. This is the evolving technology, and soon it will be studied extensively in universities also.

If there was a proper communication facility and information flow between Rikhia and Kolkata or Rikhia and Dhanbad for example, then industries and enterprises could be set up here in the villages. Deoghar would not be the automatic choice then. Currently, all the big industries are set up in cities due to availability of facilities such as transport and telephones. However, if telephones were not required, then industries would also flourish in villages, in the very interiors. Then village people would also have access to good employment, and wealth would flow out to them. They would also be able to build modern houses and develop a modern culture. At present all such things are limited to big cities the size of Delhi, Bhagalpur or Deoghar.

In the near future, information and transport technology will be such that communication with places in the far-off interiors will become easy. In Australia, for example, the ranches in the interiors do not have road access; they can only be reached by air. Their children do not go to school, but receive their learning through satellite television. Australia is a big country and it is not practical to run cables across it. We will also have to adopt similar technology with which we can connect far-off places. Imagine if you could hire a small plane at fifty rupees per head and fly seventy-five miles from Deoghar to the interiors! These developments should come about. There is no money in villages and there is no buying power there; only those who have money will spend it. For wealth to come into villages, parallel facilities will have to go there.

When I came to Rikhia, there was no telephone or electricity here. We organized underground cables, but what is needed is wireless communication. Today, computers have made everything possible and the use of this technology can change the face of villages.

In the coming years, wealth will not remain concentrated in cities. Those who have money will not want to live in the polluted cities; they will want to live in places like Rikhia. The environment of a village is clean, therefore the city dwellers will want to come to villages. To bring such people to the villages, the most important factor is communication and information. If this is available, then the wealthy will come to the villages and there will be prosperity here.

REQUIREMENTS FOR SURVIVAL

The basic requirement of a farmer is a pair of oxen, a cow, access to irrigation facilities and a house with a thatched roof. He can be a labourer, a woodcutter, a carpenter or stonebreaker ... He should have enough means to keep his children happy and to provide food for them.

The Lord spoke to me and said, "Look after your neighbours in the way I have looked after you. At least you have a hut, so give them a hut also." Therefore, I have made a resolve to

give houses, cows, rickshaws and handcarts to the destitute villagers. Most of them are farmers and farmers are very important for our wellbeing. If they revolt, the riches of the wealthy will be of no use. I do not like class conflict. All I know is that a cow, two bulls and a good source of water are a must for any farmer. They can do with an inadequate hut, but not without these other basic needs.

Food and water

The problems of the poor are poor problems, those of the millionaire are millionaire problems and those of the billionaire are billionaire problems. For a poor person, the biggest worry is obtaining food. In fact, the rich also have this worry. Whereas the poor struggle for rotis and dal, the rich worry about their bread and butter. People with even more money worry about sauce and jam. Everyone, whether rich or poor, has worries and problems. The poor man has a cough, cold, fever and diarrhoea, whereas the millionaire has a heart attack. That is the only difference.

There is a plot of land behind this place. The villagers have made a sankalpa to give this land to us. The formalities are not yet complete, and the government has to give its approval. We are going to make a big reservoir there, using the underground water resource. It will also store rainwater. It will be simple. We will draw the water with the help of pumps and send it two to three kilometres from here, or as far as possible, to the surrounding area through aluminium pipes connected with hooks. We will connect the pipes with sprinkler systems so that the water can be used for irrigation. Then the village people will have a perennial water source.

Village house

The villagers have different housing needs from townsfolk. They need more space; a flat is not adequate. In the cities one must make do with a two-room flat and a toilet, but in the villages, two-room houses are not big enough. Their houses should be spacious enough for a kitchen and keeping cows, bullocks and goats under cover, as well as storage of food for the animals, wood, cow dung or *goytha*, straw and husk. It is not possible to accommodate an entire village family in one room; separate rooms should be made for the parents, the daughters-in-law who have children, and the pregnant women. We are preparing many designs. A toilet is unnecessary; people take a small jug of water to their field and return after having looked after their needs. I want to make a system of low-cost housing for the rural people.

Employment

The need in villages is employment. The villages do not want your charity; they require a means of earning. If someone opens a factory in this region, they will open in Deoghar because the railway line, electricity lines, telephone lines, the collectorate and all such facilities are closer. They will not open it in Rikhia because transport is difficult, access to electricity is difficult. This attitude, this mode of thinking is short-sighted. If someone opens a large, two thousand million rupee industry within twenty miles of this place, the concentration in Deoghar will reduce. That will be good. The local law and order situation will improve. There are many things like these that come under re-planning which are not happening in India as yet.

The government should assist those who produce food in every way possible. That does not happen here, and that is why this country remains poor and backward. After all, one needs an incentive to work hard. People here will work hard if they receive an income corresponding to the hard work. If I spend twenty rupees and earn one hundred rupees in exchange, I will certainly work hard. The educated and the wealthy should think about this. You will have to reduce the pressure on cities. The number of cities that have developed in India is enough. There should be no more industries and no more construction in the cities of India hereafter. Stop building houses in the cities. If you want to build a house, build it in Rikhia. Come to the small villages. Small industries should also come to villages, and watch my word, in ten years India will move ahead of the US.

Cottage industries

Important requirements for the villages include small cottage industries for women. I have seen women producing articles for the market in Gujarat, Haryana and South India. There are hundreds of businesses they could start, like selling ground spices, pickles, papad. It should be an innovative idea, not bidi-making. I want them to produce things for the local market, not for the markets in Patna, Delhi or Kolkata. They can make incense sticks and thousands of other things. These people should think about what has to be done. They will listen to me and I will give them inspiration. They should produce items that I could use, the Bihar School of Yoga could use, and the people in the vicinity could use. They should be able to produce different items, but their production should not involve the use of machines to a large extent.

Cow

It is very necessary that every household in the villages has a cow. Cows give milk and compost. Even if it gives only one litre or half a litre of milk every day, the family can have a nourishing drink. Even if the farmer does not have vegetables, his family can have their rotis with milk. Meat cannot be eaten every day, and it is good if people do not eat it at all; however, milk is something they can take every day, as often as they want. Furthermore, of all the waste products in the world, only cow's dung is sacred and useful. All other types of waste, whether industrial, nuclear, human or animal, are harmful. Only cow's dung is virus-free, safe and beneficial. It can be used as a fuel for cooking and when applied fresh, as a daily floor wash, it becomes an antiseptic.

If the village people have cows, they need a bull for mating, but there is no means by which they can get a bull from Deoghar, just ten kilometres away. In the cities, we spend crores of rupees in a night, but we are neglecting the basic foundation of Indian culture.

For us, the cow is the holiest of all creatures. We consider the cow to be holier than gods. We treat cows as holier than our deities. One person in England asked why the cow in India is treated as holy. I lost my cool and retorted, "You carry dogs in your car and in India a bullock pulls a cart. You kiss your dogs, but in India, although we do not kiss the cow, we revere them, as they give us milk. Our cow is beneficial to us. You love dogs, I love cows. Your dog is a holy dog. My cow is a holy cow. Even as it is your right to kiss a dog, it is my right to worship a cow!"

Pure and auspicious environment

The environment should be pure and if we can share what we have with the village people, the atmosphere will definitely be pure and there will be a friendly relationship between us. This friendship creates a positive environment. If two people fight, a negative environment is created. Of course, on the physical level too, the air needs to be pure. However, clean air is not the only component of a good environment. *Bhavana*, feelings, are also vital components of a good environment. Sharing the joys and sorrows of others is also very necessary. If this much is done, then we will have lots of ashrams all over the country. These will have married rishis and munis living in them, who will read *Ramayana* and *Bhagavata Purana* in the morning, and then the rest of the day they will plough their fields, sell vegetables or do some other work.

The villagers should sing or listen to *Ramacharitamanas* daily. I am speaking to the villagers now. Don't tell me that you don't know how to read, because I am not asking you to read it. I am not even asking you to understand it. I am simply saying that *Ramacharitamanas* should be heard or sung daily in all village homes. That alone is sufficient.

Along with *Ramacharitamanas* you should also sing *Hanuman Chalisa*. Begin this tradition from today, if you do not already do it. Family members of all age groups, especially the children, should gather every day and sing *Ramacharitamanas* together. Those who do not know the words or cannot read should just listen. It is so easy to sing the *Ramayana*.

This practice will bring peace, plenty, prosperity and auspiciousness to your homes: the happiness of having children as well as having food to feed them, the happiness of labouring at your fields and reaping a good harvest, of keeping disease and disharmony away from your home. What happiness does one enjoy in the family apart from these?

IDENTIFYING NEEDS

One day a big acharya came here, a wealthy person. She presented something to Swami Satsangi, saying that it was a gift for my personal use. So, I told her, "Tomorrow morning buy five hundred saris, five hundred dhotis which brahmins can wear, five hundred pairs of jeans for our heroes: this is my personal need. Bring in cows, handcarts, spades, sewing machines – all these are my personal needs." What personal need do I have? I wear a langoti, a loincloth, as a courtesy to you. Today we are giving a handcart and a rickshaw as prasad. These poor labourers will now be able to earn thirty or forty rupees a day with these vehicles. Why should they beg? Whatever God gives me, I will give them. I want only a loincloth.

Social service in the villages

In the villages, people do not have proper housing or even proper drinking water facilities. They have no other alternative but to live a life of deprivation. Illiteracy is the biggest problem.

There are many people in the villages who are blind, disabled, widowed, and need help. Even after what should be retirement, at the age of fifty years, they have so much work to do that they will not even find the time to die! Therefore, instead of you retiring at the age of fifty-five or sixty, it would be better to take voluntary retirement at the age of fifty. Then run a social service institution along with ten to fifteen other people. Do not make the plan only on paper, implement it and keep it active in the villages, not in the cities, because there are many facilities in towns and cities, but none in the villages.

You may say the cities also need social services. However, the cities have many facilities, like electricity, transport, roads and telephones, but there is nothing in the villages. If educated and resourceful people focus their minds on village facilities this will indirectly help the cities, it will check population growth. When a good school opens in the village, there will be no need to send children to town to attend school. If there is a small health centre in the village, no one will need to go to the big cities for treatment. If there is a good barber, a good carpenter, a textile shop and a few other small shops in the village, no one will need to go to the cities and the pressure building up there will automatically reduce. Currently, sixty to eighty percent of the urban population comes from the villages. If you can motivate these people to return to rural life, then the cities will automatically become beautiful.

However, people will go back to the villages only when they have facilities for education and health care. This can only happen when educated people who have some resources of their own go to the villages to do social service. Social workers should go to villages, because it is necessary for people to return to a pure and natural way of life in order to find their roots and discover their real nature. This is happening everywhere in all the developed countries, such as the US and Australia; nobody stays in the cities on holidays and weekends. The roads are jammed with people travelling away from the cities to the countryside where the air is unpolluted, the environment pure, the horizon wide and clear, and the way of living relaxed and tension-free.

Safe, clean drinking water

The villages around Rikhia are pure from both the spiritual and the material point of view. There is no air or noise pollution here as in Kolkata and other cities. This place is absolutely quiet. Deep tube-well bores should be the main source of water supply here so that there is no need to depend on rains. I feel that in this area there is a huge reservoir of underground water. I have perceived this by observing the lightning. It is a well-known fact that where there are frequent episodes of thunder and lightning, there has to be a sizeable underground water resource. The frequency and magnitude of lightning episodes is far greater

here than in Munger. At times when there is lightning I feel as if it has struck right above us. It is an incredible sight, like *Star Wars*. We are trying to find out about the possibility of confirming the presence of underground water by means of satellite. We shall then be able to drill at the right point.

If we could drill a bore well of ten or twelve inches in diameter and distribute that water to nearby villages, it would be a wonderful resource. The cost of digging a water pond and drilling a tube well is the same and the villagers would be very happy not to need a pond. To fill the pond they have to rely on rainwater, but the tube well is a perennial source of water. The electricity supply here is now very efficient so we can fit a pump. We also have our own transformer, therefore there is no problem.

If we are able to extract water in large quantities, we can then convey it to the neighbouring fields, as we already have long aluminium pipes which can cover about one kilometre. Villagers can also come and bathe in that water. In the early mornings people go to bathe in rivers and ponds during the month of Kartika, so that can also be done here. We will install ten or twelve taps so that the water can flow into the fields. Then people will have safe, clean drinking water and the facility for a bath at the same place. This is what I think, and if it is God's wish then it will be done, and that will bring great relief to this impoverished area.

Practical help

A thousand houses can be constructed here in a month, but manpower is required to build a house. One person can construct one house in one month and by that time the season is over. To build a house, bricks must be made. One person has to supervise the quality of the brick-making, because if you leave it to the local people it will be hopeless. Other swamis can continue the tractor and truck loading and unloading with everybody's help.

It is necessary that dedicated people work for a period of time, offering their abilities as *nishkama seva* or karma yoga. They do not have to give all their time, just a month or two whenever they are free from their personal commitments. This can be called 'six months seasonal sannyasa', but it is not applicable to everyone. To help others you need to be qualified. When you think of helping others, it is an emotion; kindness is an emotion. In order to actually do something, emotions alone will not work. It is ability which works, and this ability must be an inherent quality. One must know about construction, one must know how to deal with human beings.

Emotion in itself is not sufficient; even money is not sufficient. When it comes to actually doing something to help others, one must be very practical. Last year we received cows, rickshaws, handcarts, sewing machines, and so forth in abundance. However, these things have not all been disposed of even now, because there are practical considerations. We have to find the right recipient for every cow. We cannot just keep on giving cows. We have to find out whether the recipient has ever kept a cow and whether he has the means to keep the cow. It takes almost one week to investigate one person.

Self-employment

Two things are very important: shelter and self-employment. Education is secondary and it is not picking up here at the pace it should, although in the last year, while I have been talking to the people, I have noticed that education has picked up a little. Parents are sending girls to school and some have even given me a hint that they want to learn English. Swami Satsangi speaks in English, so some of the girls are now jealous. It is a good thing if jealousy can work in a constructive way. This is a positive aspect of jealousy. Some of the parents have said, "We want our children to learn music and English," but I have kept quiet because, at present, that is not as important as housing and self-employment.

By self-employment I mean that the men can find work like pedalling a rickshaw or pushing a handcart, and there is sewing for the women. The villagers have started to make things and sell them, particularly the widows. I have broken the isolation of womanhood here and now they go out. Basically, all the villagers, especially the womenfolk, desire pleasure, prosperity and progeny. A better life, a better house, prosperity and children are always in their minds. Everyone wants a nice home. This floor on which we are sitting was initially rough brickwork. The village ladies saw it when they first came here to meet me. When they came again sometime later and saw marble flooring in place of the bricks, they said, "Swamiji, you have made it beautiful."

They appreciate this whole place and say, "Before, this was a wild area. Now you have made it auspicious." If they can appreciate my area, I pray to God, "May they also have similar comforts and facilities in their area." I can manage that, but the biggest problem is who will share the work? I do not want a person who comes here in the morning for eight hours duty and returns to his home in the evening. I want a person who lives here for a minimum of six months at a time. I need a civil engineer who knows construction work and the basic tenets of civil engineering.

IMPLEMENTING IMPROVEMENT

In 1993, there was a convention in Munger. I had not given any hints, but the people who came here left clothes, blankets and many other things. When they left, I did not know what to do. Somebody from Delhi sent his company truck full of clothes. So I said, "Swami Satsangi, consult the head of the village, get a list of the people and distribute the clothes and blankets as quickly as possible because I have no place to keep them." In this way, things have been changing and this change was not created by me. This change was His wish, His will.

In ancient times, the site of the ashram in Munger was called Karna Chaura. Duryodhana had made his friend, Karna, the governor of Anga Desha. His palace once stood on the site of the present Ganga Darshan ashram. Close by is the temple of the goddess Chandi, where Karna used to perform yajna followed by havan and then give gold to the brahmins. In those days the brahmins were poor. Nowadays the brahmins are cobblers in Bata and ironsmiths in Tata, but in those days they were very poor and lived only on alms.

When I came here to Rikhia, I thought, "Let this be Karna Chaura. Instead of giving gold we will give clothes, cows, huts, employment, education, and other such things." Recently, we received a truck from Orissa. Sometimes we get clothes or blankets from here and there, so our work goes on and we distribute them in the villages. Each year we give about two hundred 'good luck kits' to married girls. I thought, "Although I have not married, I can surely give dowries."

There was nothing growing when I first came to Rikhia, not even a tree, shrub or bush; this area was desolate. It was all stones. When I first came here, many villagers around us had nothing to eat in their homes. I became aware of this when Swami Satsangi told me about the pitiable conditions of the people around me. Swami Satsangi is the actual founder of this institution in every way, monetarily and administratively. When she visited the homes of the people around this ashram, only then could I understand their conditions and I thought, "My God, how do they live and survive?" She too could not fathom how they lived. One evening she returned from their homes and bemoaned, "Swamiji, I have learnt that there was no food for the night in the neighbouring home." I told her to do what she thought was best. She used to send rice, pulses, oil and condiments to such houses and people started arriving at her door.

Empowering villagers

There are rules about how charitable work should be undertaken. It has to be done in a very organized manner. If things are simply distributed in the villages, what difference will it make to anyone in the long run? Real help means enabling the villagers to generate their own strength and ability. I do not consider the poverty of this region to be a demerit. As I have said earlier, poverty exists worldwide. There is a majority of poor people all over the world; the rich are in the minority. I do not consider poverty a curse. Poverty is a curse when the poor walk the wrong path to get rid of their adversity.

Live in the villages and teach the local people some skills that will help them to improve their conditions and guide them along the right path. You can teach the women how to sew fashionable clothes in the latest styles and then find a market for these garments in the city, sell them there and send a money order back to the village. This is not charity. Charity begets poverty. In order to help people, you should make them self-sufficient; give them an opportunity to build their skills; give them autorickshaws and teach them to drive so they can earn forty or fifty rupees daily. That is more than enough for them to live on.

The purpose of Sivananda Math is not to teach yoga, nor to give mantra or other initiations. Everything here is for my neighbours: the wood, grass, fruit, water, seeds, tractors, trucks, bricks, fertilizer, cow dung, cows, cycles, underwear and saris. Nothing is mine. This place does not even give blessings. I believe that only God can give blessings, nobody else. A human being can only give good wishes. I too can only give my good wishes. I may wish you a 'Merry Christmas' or a 'Happy Diwali', but blessings can come only from God. Qualification is one thing, ability is another, but one thing is for sure: when someone gets the blessing of God, that person becomes someone. We understand that without the grace of God and without blessings, knowledge alone does not give success in life. That is what I used to tell the people of the village. So we just worship God.

Village shop

Every year on 8th September, the birthday of my guru Swami Sivananda, I pick somebody out from Rikhia panchayat and open a shop or initiate a small enterprise, a permanent business. It does not take much, only four, five or six thousand rupees to start a small village shop and stock it with things people use: detergent, pens, pencils, biscuits, clips, notebooks, and other supplies. I used to do this in Munger, too. I had a list of names of people in need of help. I would call them on my guru's birthday and ask them to open a shop to sell cosmetics, bangles, and so on. I would finance it. The shopkeeper purchases useful things from the town for the village people to buy; he makes a commission and those things become more easily available in the villages.

The first shop which Sivananda Math made for a family has a story. On 7th September, in the evening, I was inside the Akhara when a boy came to the door and said to Swami Satsangi that he had not eaten for three days. She informed me. I was surprised because his father is close to me. He is a very modest and humble man; he always hesitates to ask for anything. He is truthful and never tells lies. I often send ten or twenty kilos of rice and other grains to him. So I said to the boy's father, "Okay, use part of the verandah in the house Sivananda Math has constructed for your family and open a shop there for the village. I will provide the initial investment. I cannot give charity; I do not believe in it. You can help me and I can help you; that is all right, but no charity." So he opened a shop. We invested four or five thousand rupees, which is not much. The shop sells foodstuff and items that villagers use and we too buy our necessities from his shop. All the things are available here, so why go far? This is a good approach.

Last year I opened a shop for Lakshman Mody, who is an invalid. I met him with his daughters and enquired, "How are you doing?" He said, "Swamiji, I am doing very well." I said, "I am very happy." That night I had a very good sleep. Oh, I always have a good sleep, but that sleep was special because that man's agonies were released from my thoughts. The next day a tricycle arrived from Rajnandgaon, so I called him and said, "I have a tricycle for you. Now you will be able to purchase all your provisions from Deoghar without any problems." So, that man is now out of my mind. It seems that some karmas of agony and adversity are lurking there, but those troublesome karmas are all coming out now.

This year I gave assistance to a woman whose husband is dead. He used to make bricks for our building project. They are Muslims. I gave her seven hundred rupees and sent her with someone to Mohanpur. She bought bangles and sold them for a profit. Now she goes from house to house, sells bangles and saves the profit. Isn't it a beautiful idea that seven hundred rupees can provide employment and sustenance to someone needy? This can be done through ashrams in every state and district. If the sadhus of India were a little more aware, they could do a lot of uplifting work, but such work should only be done through personal experience and realization. No one can be forced and no one can be told to do something like this.

Now, you may say that this way of thinking is worldly, but I feel that it is spiritual because mankind is one of God's manifest forms. The whole world is God's manifest form. God is defined as nirakara and nirguna. He has no name, no caste, no home, but is this the complete definition of God? Is God only nirakara? No. God is *sakara*, with form, and *nirakara*, without form. This manifest universe, this manifest world, you, me and others, are all forms of God.

Therefore, when you are serving, helping, feeding, assisting, supporting, sympathizing and expressing compassion for others, you are actually doing something for God. There is no question of social service; this is spiritual service. God is in all the faces of those who are suffering, hungry, sick and ignored by destiny and fortune. I will be happy if you can feel love and compassion for these faces, if you can think about everyone who is less fortunate than yourself.

Employment in the village

Many jobs are provided for the working class people of nearby villages by Sivananda Math. Whatever construction work you see here has all been done by the villagers who live within two or three kilometres from here. For generator or electrical work, we call Babu next door. He gives us a connection; he installed the transformer. Our technicians are all from nearby villages, and they are artists. If the motor stops working, we send it to the contractor. He gets the motor winding done and sends it back. We do not even need to go to Deoghar. Whenever we need to buy anything from the market, we simply make a call, and they send it. We use whatever is needed; they take back the rest, and then they bill us. They send whatever is required. Does that happen in other places? No, there is supply only on prepayment.

We call the local masons *vishwakarmas,* divine builders, because they have built the ashram. The foundations, the columns and the roof are all done by these masons, as well as the outer and inner finishes. They have also installed

the electrical fittings and two transformers in our ashram. We do not need to call experts from outside to install or maintain this equipment. These masons live within a few kilometres' radius of the ashram. Electricians, carpenters and plumbers all live in the neighbourhood. The electricity and telephone were installed only after I came here and then two transformers were installed to regulate the supply. Now they have installed two dish antennas and I have a wireless telephone system, powered by that solar panel.

Our sewage system is one of the best, and has been designed and constructed by the local plumbers and masons. The water that we use is drained into underground pools and does not leave our premises.

These people also look after the horticulture and gardening. They have planted all the teak trees, the white and black sheeshams, the Assam bamboos and the neem plants. We do not plant trees for commercial purposes, but for the sake of creating greenery to maintain an ecological balance.

Agricultural society

We are starting an agricultural movement here in Rikhia. An agricultural program called *Sivananda Sarovar* has developed behind this ashram on land donated by the local people. We have already planted medicinal herbs for ordinary illnesses. Strong medicines, like antibiotics, are generally not needed here, except for emergencies. There are plenty of herbs for most of the common illnesses, like coughs and colds, stomach aches, itching and weakness. Many remedies can be prepared from ginger, onion, garlic and different types of leaves. The plants, leaves, bark, roots, flowers and fruits all have great medicinal value. Since all of us are now dependent on readymade medicines, we have forgotten practically everything about home remedies and we cannot even identify the most common medicinal plants. There may be plants growing in our own garden or in the garden next door that can be used as medicine for our illnesses, but we do not know about them.

Agriculture is a versatile culture because it provides food as well as medicines. We must encourage the rural people to revive their herbal knowledge because they can grow medicinal herbs and sell them for financial support. Many people have sent us good quality vegetable seeds from all parts of the world: Australia, Greece, and the US. Vegetables are marketable and we can grow every kind here. We also supply organic seeds to the local farmers that grow with natural fertilizers, so they do not need to use chemical pesticides.

We gave some of our exotic plants grown with foreign seeds to the agricultural college nearby. We supplied them with French mango, and now a new local variety of mango has emerged. We created a small nursery here and supplied thirty to forty thousand plants to the local people, such as mahua, mango, bamboo and rosewood. We are making a mini reservoir here, and have planted many saplings around it.

Tree plantation

We have just planted five thousand gamhar (poplar) and sheesham trees around the panchayat. Many more saplings have been given to the villagers and I have asked them to plant and nurture them.

There are more than forty-five species of Australian eucalyptus trees. The trees growing here belong to one of them. I can go on cutting and harvesting this Australian species. After four years, when they became too thick, I cut them down to about one metre and gave them to my neighbours to use in their house construction. In a few years, we will have another crop and I will again cut them down. In this way, I can get four crops from each tree. Initially, I planted about five to six hundred trees and I have already given away about half the wood.

Construction skills

Sivananda Math has received a tractor and a truck. We use these for collecting sand from the river, as we do not purchase sand for the construction work. A lady arrived from France who knew how to make bricks and we procured coal from Dhanbad and used it to fire the bricks here for the construction of houses in the villages. Then we realized that the bricks made at Sultanganj were cheaper and harder than the ones we prepared here, so we decided to procure bricks from Sultanganj. Sultanganj bricks are so strong and long-lasting that ten-inch-thick walls are not necessary; even five-inch-thick walls will carry the weight of the foundation.

One of the swamis, who has been living here for several years, knows about woodwork, carpentry, masonry and electrical work. When the wooden furniture gets old and has been damaged by weevils, she knows which insecticides to use to prevent further damage. She learnt these skills from her father with whom she used to work. She is quite young, and enjoys her work. Today, a new house is being built in a nearby village and she has gone to mark out the plot. It takes two months or more to build one house. A civil engineer is also needed for the construction work, to decide on the area, how to make the pillars, where to put the rods, the structure of the foundations, the height of the plinth, and so on. All these details have to be looked at in the proper way. To do good works requires great skill and expertise.

Making compromises

If every Indian decides to make one family self-dependent, then I think that many problems of India will be solved. This problem cannot be solved by the government. I have been observing this for forty to fifty years. This can be done only by us. When one rich man goes to a hill station for a holiday, he spends forty to fifty thousand rupees. If he decides not to go to a hill station one year, what is the problem? In this way, if each person with means makes a few compromises in his luxury expenditure, we ourselves can solve the social problem of India, which the government has been unable to do. Bhartrihari has said, "Charity, enjoyment and destruction are the three channels of wealth. To the one who neither gives nor enjoys, the third will inevitably happen."

Our duty is to share our extra wealth with the poor. Bringing assistance to the villages will help ease the situation that exists in the big cities, because the poor in the cities are migrants from the villages. If the situation in the villages improves, migration to the cities will decrease and so will the population there. This will improve the crime situation that exists in the cities; theft, robbery, hooliganism and fraud will lessen. When migrant labourers are unable to make ends meet, they grab in whatever manner they can. What we need is ruralization, but the emphasis is on urbanization. The atmosphere and social structure of a city are totally different from that of a village.

People need hard work
In Deoghar you will find rickshaws and handcarts with 'Presented by Sivananda Math' written on the back. The town is just flooded with them. In China there is a proverb,

"If you come across a poor man, don't just give him fish, which will only serve as his dinner. Instead, teach him how to fish so that he can feed himself for the rest of his life." I also think like that. Charity is the mother of poverty. Thoughtless charity or too much charity brings about more poverty, although charity may be necessary in a time of calamity, such as earthquake, drought or flood.

We may give a bicycle, but that is not a donation. I am strictly against donations, charity or alms. Begging for alms is the duty of a sannyasin, not that of a *grihastha*, or householder. A sannyasin has to beg, he cannot donate. A grihastha does not beg, he offers things in charity. I cannot make the river flow back upstream. By God's grace, Ganga is flowing in the right direction down here. I am not Ganga or God, but there must be a medium of expression for God's grace. Therefore, we offer everything that people donate to God: rickshaws, bicycles, tools, even cows and bulls. These become offerings just like flowers or sweets, and then we distribute them as prasad. There is no stamp of donation on them; they are the Lord's prasad. When worship begins, we offer prasad to the village people.

A society that lives on charity is not a healthy one. Society needs hard-working people. I am surrounded by labourers, working class people. The people of this district have decided to increase the yield of rice and wheat. They have been making an effort in this direction since last year and so we are now boring a well, which will be forty to fifty feet deep and will touch a perennial source of water for their crops. We are also distributing high quality seeds for their vegetable farming. Let us see how long it will take to show results. God took millions of years to create this universe, to make it what it is today. I do not know how long this local creation will take to fructify.

Garlands of giving

A few days ago, a boy came to see me one evening and said, "Swamiji, you are having a celebration here and I want to sell garlands." I said, "Okay", and asked him how many and at what price. He replied, "Ten or fifteen, only two rupees each." The next day he brought fifteen to twenty garlands, which I distributed to the guests, and they looked wonderful.

In the evening, I paid him fifty rupees and he burst into tears. When I asked him why he was crying, he said, "Swamiji, you have given my family fifty rupees." I also dissolved into tears and said, "God, why don't you give me good ideas? Why do you only give me all kinds of funny religious ideas?" So, He gave me this idea to buy all the garlands in this area for two square miles. I have asked Swami Niranjan to tell every boy to pick fifty flowers, thread them all on a string and bring them here by twelve o'clock so that I can give a garland to everyone. That is one thousand garlands for one thousand people. This is not to welcome you, nor is it to give you my good wishes. I am being very frank. I want to give these boys two rupees a garland so that their kitchen smells of food, so that these children can sleep well.

Every day I give away one or two thousand garlands. What do I have to do with this giving and taking of garlands? Do I become great by offering these garlands? If you offer me a big garland will I become great? No. One garland costs six rupees and one poor man earns six rupees each time you buy a garland. Buy one thousand garlands and give him six thousand rupees. Get the six thousand from someone. If they are thieves, we are also thieves, always taking from one another, so what difference does it make?

Yes, you are a thief, I am a thief, and everyone is a thief. It is the truth. If you give a part of your pilfering to me, I will transfer it to others. People from different churches send me cash or its kind. The International Church sends things. Swamis from other countries and different religions around the world send me money for many, many cows and tell me to donate them to the needy.

Contentment in serving

This year (1994), as the planets moved into position, the swamis took the tractor into the villages and ploughed about one hundred to one hundred and fifty acres of land.

I asked the swamis to do an efficient job with the tractor, so they left at six every morning and ploughed all day. In the evening, when they returned covered in wet mud, I asked them how they felt, "Contented," they replied. They find contentment in service to others. The village people all around my place are very happy. It is important that your neighbours should be as happy as you are. Someone from Dhanbad brought the tractor and left it at the gate. I do not know who gives what; people just leave things here out of kindness. Everything is possible where there is goodwill.

Training to keep cows
Cows are given to those who want to improve their lot. A cow is brought and kept here in the name of a villager. Then a family member of that villager, his wife, sister, daughter or somebody else comes morning and evening to look after it. They carry out whatever service is necessary for the cow's upkeep such as milking, cutting the fodder and cleaning the cowshed. They are trained for one month in tending the cow. If the cow has any health problems then a vet is consulted. A sannyasin from Bilaspur has come to give veterinary training and consultations in treating any health problems. Now there are two milch cows that give abundant milk, about twelve to fifteen litres a day.

After one month, the villagers take the cow away to their homes. During this one-month training period, there is a good daily supply of milk and milk products: kheer, cottage cheese, paneer, curd, kadhi. Dairy products have replaced vegetables. On the first day there is wheat porridge; on the second day, milk and rice; on the third day, curd and rice; on the fourth day, rotis with paneer kofta; and on the fifth day, cottage cheese. I think the best *daan*, or gift, is that of a cow. Go on donating cows.

Implementing positive thoughts
The idea of helping others is very easy to have, but when it comes to implementing it, then the difficulties arise, despite being a renunciate. Here, within three days my store was full, but to distribute everything requires time and planning. We have to make a list of every member of each household in every village: who is the head, who is the son, who is the daughter, who is getting married, what their ages are. This information is inputted into the computer and then family bundles are made according to the details on the list. When the prasad bundles are ready for a village it gets distributed by trucks, tractors and cars. Plenty of manpower is required for this work. It takes more than three days to prepare bundles for one village and that too is done with the help of

the local people. Thus, helping others is not an easy job. It requires organizational skills and so many great qualities.

Thinking of others may be a very good quality but it hardly requires any talent, 'Let everyone be happy' – how long does it take to think that? It takes no time or skill to feel that. Your thoughts are very good and you have prayed for everyone to be happy, but what have you actually done? To implement that positive thought you should live like a sannyasin for a few days. Sannyasa has only one dharma: to work for the welfare of others. Once I asked a lady who came here, "How do you sleep?" She replied, "I stitch all the torn saris together, spread them on the floor and sleep." She was a very sick and weak woman. Recently I sent her to have a gall bladder operation. These are the practical points of spiritual life.

You must understand that saints are not born merely for salvation, for gaining knowledge or for worship. Saints are born for the welfare of others and that is their only work. This is written in the *Bhagavad Gita* as well. You will obtain two advantages from this. One advantage is that others will benefit. The other is that you will realize that one can live like a sannyasin as well as manage the household, run the factory, industry or even the government. You can do everything more efficiently when you live like a sannyasin with the feeling of dedication and non-attachment. Every action can be done in the spirit of sannyasa.

Of course, I am not a reformer; it is the dharma of saints and sages to make people sing the Lord's name, to put them on the correct path, to make them tread the path of dharma, to give them the knowledge of discrimination and of the Vedas. Besides this, they should distribute cows and bulls in the villages and make arrangements for a regular water supply. The dwellings in which they live need not be of cement. After all, where were all the Vedas, Puranas and smritis written? In forests and in thatched huts while sitting on the ground. And they are considered to be the greatest masterpieces in the world today.

God in suffering humanity

Try to see God in suffering humanity. This is the duty of saints, sages and holy men, as well as householders. It is the duty of humanity. Today there is so much pain and misery everywhere because God is not seen where He actually is, in suffering humanity. Therefore, your spiritual endeavour will fail. You will find peace of mind in the temples, but that is not the ultimate in life.

Peace of mind is very private and personal; it is not the ultimate goal of human life. As long as the world, society, the cities, towns and villages are not peaceful, the Earth will not enjoy peace. That is why the ancient rishis, munis, seers and thinkers have found *shanti*, peace, everywhere and not only in temples: *Dyauh shantih, antariksham shantih* – "May the sky be peaceful, may the atmosphere be peaceful." When you visit a temple you get personal peace. When you go for darshan of Swami Satyananda you feel very happy. This is good, but it is a very personal thing.

Personal shanti may be an aim, but it cannot be your ultimate aim in life. You have to search for that peace which surpasses all understanding and which embraces every living creature. You have to search for God; you have to find Him in the alleys, lanes and houses. For that reason, I told the swamis to visit all the houses and look after the people there. I told them not to go empty-handed, to take the prasad bundle we have prepared for them. You never know, the Lord may be hiding in any house. So, take prasad of blankets with you, take saris for the womenfolk, take jeans or dhotis for the men, take toys for the children, take a few pots and pans, even aluminium will do.

We are working for rural development. Of course the whole of India is our county, but all the work will be done first for Rikhia panchayat. All the members of this Rikhia panchayat are my disciples and every girl is my disciple. The entire panchayat is my ashram. I have made each household my household. Their pains and pleasures are my own. Their poverty is my poverty and their happiness is my happiness. If anyone is sick, it is my ashram inmate who is sick. That is not a social philosophy, it is vedantic philosophy. The philosophy is very simple: you have to see yourself in everyone and you have to see everyone within your own self. I am teaching you the theme of Vedanta. It is written as *atmabhava* in Vedanta.

RIKHIA: A WAY TO SERVE

To please God you must serve the poor, the destitute, the disabled, the sick, the hungry, the naked and the helpless. You must love the orphans who are loved by no one. Be the servant of the downtrodden, the poorest of the poor and the lowest among the lowly. If you want to please God, serve him in the poor, the helpless and the sick. You don't have to go to a temple or church. You don't have to become a swami, sannyasin or yogi. You don't have to practise asana, pranayama or meditation. Just do whatever you can with your mind, knowledge, influence and might, to help the poorest of the poor, the lowest of the low. God will not be pleased if you only fill your own pocket. God loves those who love Him in this form.

Many years ago, during a Kumbha mela, a man suffering from leprosy was brought to the ashram in a gunny bag. Swami Sivananda called me and said, "Put him in a room and clean his body with the necessary antiseptics." Swamiji was a doctor and he knew what to do. I also had a little knowledge about such matters. I am not a regular doctor, but I know as much as a regular doctor. So I carried out the duty I had been given. That man was obnoxious: his smell, his attitude, his behaviour, his entire being was something which I could not accept.

The next morning when I gave Swamiji a report, he asked me how the man was. I said, "Swamiji, that man is so difficult, his disease, his sores are so difficult." Swamiji replied, "You want to find God without any effort. You want to realize God without a change of heart, mind, philosophy and concept, without destroying your personal nest. You

have a personality, character, views, habits, likes and dislikes. Destroy them first and change your heart." If it had been a beautiful young lady, I would have served her without complaining. Even if it had been a young man, a beautiful or rich man, I would have served him. Such a man was I! Do you think I was fit to realize God? No, I was unfit.

On the day I heard God's command, "Love thy neighbours. Help them as I have helped you", that scene, and what Swamiji had told me, came into my mind: "You want to realize God without changing yourself. You want to see the light without operating upon your own cataract. No, it is not possible." At that time, another realization dawned also. For many years I had been searching for the answer to a question. I pray to God and repeat His name; everybody does it. I like to remember Him, like everybody else. Now the problem comes. How do I love Him?

Do good to others
Serve the poor and suffering, and motivate others to do the same. This is also a convertible currency. Seventy-five percent of your karmas will become pooja; the remaining twenty-five percent you can leave to God. Then your karmas will be seventy-five percent pure and only twenty-five percent will be adulterated. Even a twenty-four carat gold coin contains some copper. Without that, no ornament can be made. Let this twenty-five percent adulteration remain, because without it you and your family cannot survive. Thus, the ratio should be fifty percent guru seva, twenty-five percent service to the poor and downtrodden, and the remaining twenty-five percent for the welfare of your family. Then your karmas will be transformed into worship. This I am telling each one of you. You are being given such a good opportunity to gain virtue. It is your good fortune that instead of giving only to your own, you can give to so many. Hold fast to your faith in God.

I am only repeating what the scriptures have preached. One path is to repeat the name of God and the second sadhana is to do good to others. This is the simplest and easiest path in Kali Yuga. I am not the first to tell you this. These are the only two ways. Practise repeating God's name for a short period of time, either verbally or mentally, with a mala. You can say, "*Om Namah Shivaya, Om Namah Shivaya,*" "*Sri Rama, Sri Rama,*" "*Jesus, Jesus, Jesus,*" "*Holy Mary.*" It is up to you. I am not giving you initiation; I am only making a suggestion. In addition, do good to others and your mirror will begin to clean itself. One day you will see yourself very clearly and exclaim in realization, "Oh, I am Brahman." Worship and devotion pave the way to oneness with God.

Do not turn away a beggar

If an educated, well-dressed man comes to your door, you offer him a chair and greet him with a handshake, but when a naked and hungry beggar comes to your door, you kick and abuse him. You have an altogether different way of behaving. Sometimes a poor widow comes to me seeking help. Swami Satsangi tries to enquire into her situation to find out the truth. I think that even though she may not be telling the entire truth, even though she may have some money in the bank, no Indian woman can be untruthful about being a widow. No Indian woman can tell a lie about her husband's death. I just tell Swami Satsangi not to waste her time making unnecessary enquiries and to make good use of the money she has by buying the poor widow a sewing machine.

You have to find a place in your heart for people who are not known to you. You have to act out your compassion and feelings on behalf of these people. Consolation by words only is not enough: "Oh see, he is full of sorrow, look what karmas he has got!" That is nothing. At least give him a glass of tea. Don't turn away the beggar at your gate. Some people say, "Nowadays all these people have turned wicked." This is not right. That philosophy is only to defend your own petty mind. Think about whether what I am saying is right or wrong and apply your own reasoning. If I am not right then leave it, but nobody, however wicked he may be, will come begging at your gate to cheat you. I am telling you honestly. I have lived that life, which is why I can speak from my own experience. People used to say that I was cheating everyone. Maybe even now people are saying, "Look, how much he is cheating!"

I am not joking. Never refuse a beggar at the gate of your house. Keep puffed rice, onions, and some salt. If there is no cooked food ready, then give him puffed rice on a leaf plate. It is no good wailing, "Oh God, he has come to my door!" After all, he is a beggar. He has a soul and that soul is in you too. The soul, the light that is inside the beggar is the same light that is in you. The electricity in one bulb is the same electricity in another bulb. It is the same electricity in Deoghar and Mumbai. The same soul is in everyone, only the circuits are different. Your circuit is different from my circuit, so when I turn on the switch my light is on, not yours. The circuits are different, aren't they? What is that circuit? Ego, the circuit of individuality. If ego is effaced then when my light is on, everyone's light goes on and if my light is off then everyone else's goes off.

Respect His creation
You ought to give attention to those people who are completely neglected by society, whom nobody bothers about. If you cast a helpful eye towards such people, God will turn His grace towards you. This is not only what Satyananda preaches, all the holy books, the Bible, Koran, *Ramayana* and Vedas, tell us this. Christ, Mohammed, Sri Krishna, Mahatma Gandhi and all the great teachers have said the same thing. God is called *deenabandhu*, friend to the unfortunate, helpless and lowly. Have you ever read about an *amirbandhu* God, who is friend to the rich and fortunate? If you believe that God is a friend to the poor, then you should play the role of benefactor to the poor. In this way, you and God will become very close to each other.

The poor people of the world are a challenge to your spiritual life, whether in Asia, Africa or anywhere else in the world. There are people suffering mentally, physically and economically. What percentage of your income are you spending on them? One bottle of liquor costs a minimum of one hundred rupees and it evaporates within no time. A single doctor's bill is nothing less than three hundred rupees. Similarly, people complain that cigarettes have become very expensive and yet they smoke their money away. Pass up on these things just for a day and divert that expenditure to the poor and needy. You are ready to spend everything on yourself, but you are not prepared to spend one dollar on a poor man, and still you talk about God! No. You have to respect His creation, His maya.

Do not underrate it. I am not talking of charity. I am talking about the absolutely classical spiritual system and believing in that. You are not jokers, all of you are seekers. Think a little about others. Have at least some corner in your heart for the suffering and misery of others. If you help your fellow beings even a little, God will most certainly shower His grace upon you. This is a sadhana, a spiritual practice in itself. There are innumerable poor widows in our villages. They have no future, no life of their own. Their existence is meaningless. They have neither bhoga nor yoga before them. They are made to feel useless. Widows come in the condemned category. This is the state of society that I am pointing out to you.

Find a way to serve

Have you ever given a thought to reforming society, to making it better by serving the poor and needy? How can you serve the poor, the poorest of mankind? Who will tell you all this? You have to find out how to serve. As you know, money has three destinations: *daan*, offering; *bhoga*,

enjoyment; and *nasha*, destruction. All property has these three destinations only. You may enjoy it or you may offer it, otherwise it will be lost or destroyed: anything and everything, movable or immovable, gold or silver, food or sweetmeats, clothes or animals, cars or anything else.

Think about how much you need for your own enjoyment, "How can I wear so many clothes?" "What will I do with these gold and silver ornaments?" To collect and keep things is not enjoyment; to store things is also not enjoyment. Enjoyment is utilizing things for oneself. You may require a life of comfort and for that you may need a refrigerator, an air conditioner, a good television set, a heater, a hot water geyser and so on, but besides these you have many other things that you do not need and such things you must offer to the needy. This should not be done as charity. If you offer a job or service to the needy, or if you make a firm arrangement for the livelihood of a needy person, you will be doing yeoman service.

Ten percent of your income must be spent on God's creation, otherwise, do not talk about God. Ten percent of thirty days is three days. Whatever you spend on your own enjoyment and luxuries for three days should go to the poor. Abstain from these pleasures just for three days per month. Some people enjoy non-vegetarian food, some enjoy eggs, some go to see movies, and some enjoy themselves in other ways. They spend four or five hundred rupees easily on their enjoyment and pleasure in a day. Three days' expenses would amount to fifteen hundred rupees or so. Divert this money for the education of a poor child and help the lame to walk. Spend one or two thousand rupees on a blind man so that he can have his eyes operated on. Maybe he can regain his sight. Pick up a leper from the street and find a house for him. Helping others is the easiest way to liberate oneself. Serving others is the easiest way to free oneself from bondage. Step out of your selfish boundaries. Think a little about others.

Your heart should be so soft, so tender, and so sensitive, that it should immediately respond to the cries of agony and pain from others. You should be able to feel the pain of other people, to feel the tragedy in another's life. Before you are able to experience Brahman or the Lord, to see the light or experience enlightenment, you must be able to feel the pain and agony of another person. If you cannot feel or respond to another's agony mentally, it means you cannot attain peace, you cannot see the light. A compassionate and sensitive heart, which feels and responds to another's pain, attains knowledge effortlessly. The more distant and unaffected you are from the suffering and distress of others, the further Brahman will be from you. God, Shiva, Rama, Devi, all will be beyond your reach. Spiritual life without compassion is useless; it will get you nowhere. Only those with such tender hearts can feel and experience the paramatma.

There was a driver with this ashram who stayed with us for two or three years. Then we arranged an autorickshaw for him and now he is self-sufficient and earns his own living of one hundred rupees a day. If he fails to earn his living after we have made these arrangements, we can do little because it is due to fate. We were satisfied that we did what had to be done. If a labourer earns forty or fifty rupees a day, it is not very much. No one earning in this meagre way is capable of making both ends meet. It is the duty of each one of us, be it the ruler or the ruled, to see that no one is deprived of this basic minimum need.

If you want to attain nirvikalpa samadhi, savikalpa samadhi, bhava samadhi or samadhi of any type, damned or blessed, if you want to have a vision of divinity, then find a way to serve the poor. Your body, blood, soul, youth, wealth, intelligence, everything should be geared to serving and raising mankind to a proper position. You should not aspire only for your own meditation, communion or moksha. You should rethink about spiritual life and reschedule your program. The next time I call you, I may ask you to make roads. So come prepared with spades, axes and such tools. I will call you all here and ask you to make roads in the interior where there are no roads. If you do not want to work, then do not come.

It is not wrong to do pooja or to read the *Ramayana*, Bible or Koran. It is not wrong to visit a church, mosque or temple. It is not wrong to seek *satsang*, the holy company of sadhus and sannyasins, but the most important worship of God is to see him in his world of creation. After all, Vishnu is omnipresent. He pervades the whole earth. God, You are immanent in everything. You are present in all forms of manifestation. You are there in the mango trees, in the water and in the soil. Water is present everywhere in the form of all created beings. Air, fire and space are also everywhere. Similarly, God is present everywhere. Think this over carefully.

Take care of others

"God, give me enough so that I can give to others" – let this be your prayer. Do not pray only for your own television set and motor cycle. If you seek peace of mind and salvation for yourself, it will not come because all around you there are problems, anxieties and restlessness; everyone is unhappy. How can you be happy when the whole world is unhappy? The whole world is burning and you are seeking your own peace and salvation. Therefore, first take care of others, and then take care of yourself. First take care of their moksha, and then your moksha is guaranteed. First take care of their peace and prosperity, and then your peace and prosperity are guaranteed. If you cannot think about others, if you cannot understand the problems of others, you can never realize yourself.

This is the sum and substance of all religions, the message of all saints. I know this very well because He spoke to me, to my inner soul. I have heard the voice of God. Christ heard it; I also hear it. I am not a second Christ, mind you, not a pontiff nor a teacher. I am a servant of God. Yes, a servant of God. I have that feeling and I do not have to prove it to anyone. There is no question of self-realization. I am not here for self-realization. I am not here for acquiring *siddhis* or spiritual attainments. I am not here to live a very divine, spiritual or religious life. I did come here for that, but that is not my attitude any more.

Share your wealth

A life of comfort and luxury is a suicidal life. A simple life is a good and balanced life. Do not be affected by riches. Dollars cannot create destiny, dollars cannot create personality. If you do not listen to the message you are being reminded of today, a day will come when the desperate unfortunates increase from thirty to seventy percent, then your life will be in peril. Thieves, dacoits and vagabonds will kidnap your children and terrorize you into signing cheques for large amounts of money in their names. This is not something that will take place in the distant future. It is already happening in many countries. Therefore, I am cautioning you. When I am explaining a spiritual truth, I tend to talk about social and worldly matters as well. I am talking of that reality which will help your society. If there is heat, fire, disaster and death all around and you alone live in an air-conditioned room, how long can you survive? So, you must try to improve the conditions outside your family. The world exists beyond your wife, husband and children. The solution is not 'we two and our two'. This idea must come into focus.

You must think about the population that is much less fortunate than you and do something for these miserable ones who are weak, sick, poor, lame, crippled and handicapped. You must think ahead. What I am saying has a deep social significance and a political purpose as well. I am not just chatting casually to you. I have a share in your fortunes. By this, I do not mean my physical entity. I love one and all without exception. I am not a limited individual. I was born with a destiny to fulfil. My guru told me everything about my mission and myself. Therefore, I am claiming one of your pockets. Let the other be with you, but one of your pockets belongs to me. One pocket belongs to you and the other belongs to mankind. Have one bank account for your family and another account for mankind. Divide your money, wealth and fortune. Divide your good luck and let me have a portion of it. That means, let mankind have it; otherwise, you will have social problems. All over the world, there are millions of blind, lame, deaf and dumb people. There are millions of orphans and destitute children. There are so many poor who need a helping hand. There are so many sick that need your love and care. Jesus said this. Today you swear in his name, but what did you do during his time? You crucified him. He came to save, to redeem. He gave you this message; I am not saying it for the first time. It was pronounced two thousand years ago and Christians must remember this. This is my practical advice to you.

IMPRESSIVE CHANGES

Today, Rikhia is slowly entering the 21st century. We have PCOs, mobile networks, satellite connections, cybercafés, internet, shops, traffic, and even nice, bright, well-dressed children in school uniforms going to school and ladies wearing nice saris and woollens in winter. Do you remember how it was here when I first came to Rikhia in 1989?

During the day, no one would pass this way. Nowadays at least fifty to a hundred scooters pass by. This man, Tetu Ramani, is the *pradhan*, the chief of this village and this area. The land where the *sarovar*, the reservoir, has been constructed was donated by him. He said that before we came, the people here did not eat every day. They would only get proper food once in three days. He said that his eldest daughter has seen starvation whereas the daughters who were born after I came here eat well. This was just one aspect of their plight and condition when I arrived here. The ladies did not even have enough cloth to cover their bodies! If you enter a colony and the ladies are not clad properly due to poverty, what does it mean? They are still living in the primitive age. You should have seen the boys and girls of Rikhia before.

We have constructed 'Annapoorna Kshetram' to feed all the kanyas and batuks. It was donated by a public sector company of India, Bokaro Steel Plant. Bokaro Steel renovated the building at its own expenses, and it is now ready. In the coming years the children will not need to ask their mother for food; the ashram will provide it. The ashram will provide their nutrition because it is the duty of society to look after its children. It is the duty of society; it is not the duty of government or of NGOs. It is the duty of the entire society, and I am society.

Today, there is no family in this panchayat which goes without food. There is no child in this panchayat who does not get a proper dress every one or two months. On every festival, whether it is Holi, Diwali, Dussehra, Navaratri or Guru Poornima, we give them beautiful dresses. We always have supplies ready for them. When the children of this panchayat get five or six sets of dresses every year, what will you call them? Destitute? Lower middle class? Upper middle class? In which category do we place them? They are happy and their prosperity is percolating. Prosperity should always percolate, because that keeps a man in check. If riches come like tsunami, they completely sweep you away and you cannot control yourself.

Today, the children speak English, chant in Sanskrit impeccably and have developed many other talents. They are full of surprises. Some of the girls even go by bicycle to Deoghar to study at college. The change is very apparent. The parents too have undergone a transformation. They are comfortable and happy, not in dire need as they were when I came in 1989. This change has taken place not because we have given them many things, but because the children, the kanyas and batuks who come here have somehow brought prosperity to their families.

The kanyas have attracted prosperity to their homes. God alone knows how they have done it, but they have successfully attracted Lakshmi into their homes. Next year, I will introduce them to solar lamps so they can study in the evenings, since it is not possible for everybody to have electricity. We are trying to find out about solar lamps and have experimented with many different types. We have solar lamps that don't need any battery, switch or panels. They are very simple. You just fix them in the ground, they charge from the sun the whole day long and when it begins to get dark, they light up. This works well here because the sun is very strong. If we can provide one or two to each family, they will be able to light up their courtyards. It will act as a bright *diya*, lamp, that will burn the whole night long. For the village and poor folk, this is sufficient. They will not need kerosene oil or lamps any more.

Gradually, the people here are becoming aware that they can also become self-sufficient. I am not saying that they can become millionaires, but a farmer should be able to lead a comfortable life. He should be able to afford a glass of milk for his children. Children need milk. If he can't do that, it is a disgrace to our dharma. What are the saints and great souls of India doing? If all their energy was utilized then there would be no need for any government. The saints and great souls of this country are very powerful. Each jagadguru could look after a state. We would have a battalion of people behind us. Actually, we are the rulers of this country, but we keep a very low profile because we do not want to enter politics. We do not want to be involved in any hanky-panky. Nor do we want to include politicians in the spiritual movement, as we do not need them.

In ten years, great change has taken place in the entire panchayat. Now, every family has been supplied with a bicycle, umbrellas, something to eat and something to wear. We have touched their agriculture, households and every aspect of their life. Previously, these village people were completely forsaken non-entities whom nobody cared for. The government did not take care of them and they were unable to take care of themselves. They had no water for irrigation. Since then, the change has taken place and within a short period this will become a happy and prosperous area.

Yes, we are working for rural development and all the work will be done first for Rikhia panchayat. Of course the whole of India is our panchayat, but once we start here others will also understand how good work for humanity is possible, and how good people from faraway places can meet each other and share their knowledge and skills.

CULTURAL DEVELOPMENT IN RIKHIA

Two cradle ceremonies

We celebrate Jhoolan every year here at Rikhiapeeth in the name of Sri Krishna who, according to history, was born almost five thousand years ago on the banks of the river Yamuna at Mathura in India. *Jhoola* means cradle or swing, and *jhoolan* means cradle or swing ceremony. Just as two intimate friends sit together on a swing in the rainy season and enjoy themselves, in the same way Radha and Krishna are placed on the jhoola or swing and devotees get a chance to swing them. Or, just as you put a baby in a cradle and swing him so he enjoys it and is happy, in the same way baby Krishna or Gopala Krishna is placed on the jhoola and everyone gets a chance to swing him. We have two jhoolas, one for baby Krishna and the other for the young Krishna and his playmate, Radha.

We have been having this ceremony for the village folk since I came here. You may have seen them last night, how they come in large numbers and are full of excitement and fervour for this event. In the monsoon season, every village house in India has a jhoola in which they keep Krishna, such is their faith in this ceremony. This is a simple down-to-earth way to remember Sri Krishna, the greatest man ever born in India. Krishna is a historical figure, the history of this land cannot be written without his mention.

History becomes legend and survives only because it is transmuted into legend. Legend does not die because it is embedded in the hearts and minds of the simple people who do not care much for politics. Krishna has become a legend; now no one can wipe him out of our hearts. Wherever we go, we take him with us. No matter who rules, he stays with us. You will remember my words. Only the history which becomes legend lives on. History dies, but legends live. Those legends then become fantasy and dreams. This is what you have seen here in Rikhia last night, a fantasy, a beautiful dream coming alive.

We have another cradle ceremony in the month of December. On the 24th, Christmas Eve, and the 25th, Christmas Day, we celebrate Christmas, the birth of Christ. So, each year Rikhia has two cradle ceremonies, one for baby Krishna in August and the other for baby Christ in December. For Krishna, we have an Indian cradle and for Christ we have an Italian cradle brought from Rome. The Italian devotees brought it for the ceremony.

Finally, remember, India is the cradle of Christianity. I believe in being a good Christian. I am a sannyasin who belongs to the Shaiva tradition, but I am a devotee of Rama who is the icon of the Vaishnava tradition. I worship Krishna too, and every year, I worship Devi during the Sat Chandi Yajna. After that, during Christmas I worship Christ in the kutir I have built for Him. So, what harm is there if you are a Christian and go to a Shiva temple, or if you go to a Rama or a Vishnu temple, or if you worship Shakti? You still remain a Christian and I remain a Hindu.

The idea of Christ Kutir is a brand new one. No Christian institution in India has a Raghunath Kutir, and no mandir, temple or ashram has a Christ Kutir. Rikhia is the only place where both Raghunath and Christ are worshipped under the canopy of one institution. We will certainly not build a church here. This is a cottage for Christ, a little house where he will live. Everyone has a cottage, so Christ should have a cottage. A place where Christ can be worshipped along with Raghunath is only possible in India because of the religious tolerance that exists within the people here.

5

People Development

CHILDREN

I arrived here in 1989, on 23rd September. Now it is 2009, so I have been in Rikhia for twenty years. Since then the ashram has been successful in looking after the children of Rikhia panchayat.

At Rikhia, we have adopted almost five to six thousand young boys and girls, *kanyas* and *batuks*, virgins and celibates. All day long, they swarm around the ashram like bees. They only go home at night; their huts are not very inspiring, as they are poor people. These poor, humble, simple, innocent and meek children are all the blessed children of Rikhia who were born after I came to live here. These children never see me because I live in seclusion. It is Swami Satsangi who arranges everything for them and interacts with them. She has been doing this for the past eighteen years.

The children here are down-to-earth; they are practical. They do not know how to get tired, they have no concept of fatigue and exhaustion. Here in Rikhia, you can find a jubilant atmosphere throughout the year. You are lucky to be here. It is a joy to be with children. If I was married I would have had only two or three, but as a sannyasin I have so many. I am enjoying my paternity! I am a father without paying the tax!

They are very brilliant, very intelligent children. Their parents are not here as they work in Deoghar, Asansol, Dhanbad, and so on. Only the mothers and grandmothers live here and look after the children. The children say the ashram is their first home. All the children come to class here every day. They have English, yoga, kirtan, *Bhagavad Gita*, *Ramayana* and computer classes. Go to any ashram in India. Go to any religious place in the world. You will not find so many children participating in the most serious ceremonies anywhere unless there is Michael Jackson or Madhuri Dixit, but they will not come for *Ramayana*. Only older people will come.

Our karma, our duty

You will find the children sometimes in blue dress, sometimes in red, sometimes in jeans, sometimes in tracksuits, sometimes in skirts and blouses. They have been coming here since 1989. Many have graduated; many are now married and even have children. Many have gone to Kolkata, Mumbai, Pune, Asansol, everywhere in India. Rikhia is spread all over now. In another fifty years, it will spill all over the world, because children are the future of earth.

If the children are groomed properly in a free atmosphere, with free expression and a good environment, they will create a new earth, a new society, and Rikhia is an example of this. You call it religion, I accept it. You call it spirituality, all right. You call it mysticism, occultism, okay. And if you call it joy and recreation, perfect! Everything is here. We do not know what the future of these children is. It lies in the hands of God. We are doing our karma, our duty. It is said that: "It is the duty of society to look after children up to the age of twelve'" – *Dwadash varshe bhavet Gauri*. After twelve, the parents should look after them; after sixteen or eighteen, the wife or husband should look after them; after fifty or sixty, their children should look after them. However, up to twelve it is the duty of society to look after their education, their health and everything else. I am society so it is my duty to care for these children.

These children have received samskaras. Their inner self has received samskaras. I want to open their minds, to evolve their consciousness, to unfold their emotions so that they live their life with honesty and devotion. Who knows, some Shankaracharya, Mohammed, Christ or Ramakrishna may appear from among them!

Computer and *Bhagavad Gita* classes
They speak very good English. Originally, the classes started with just one girl, Ruby Ramani from Nawadih village, and now there are so many. I think they, as well as their parents, are very happy. One thing is very important; we do not deal with anyone in the village except the children. Through them we deal with the entire family.

We have a very good computer section and this year a hundred kanyas will learn computers, here at the ashram. In two months they can learn what students in the big cities take two years to learn because of the supportive environment. The older ones among them have started teaching the younger ones. Their maximum age is thirteen. In this ashram, we allow village girls only up to the age of thirteen. After thirteen, they retire to make way for more children. People say, what is the point of their learning computers if they have to get married and collect cow dung in the morning? I say, even educated people can collect cow dung. In the villages of European countries, there are educated people who live the life of a farmer, a cleaner, a cook, a driver or servant.

We have started Sanskrit classes for the boys. All these little scoundrels are studying the *Bhagavad Gita*. They are so energetic, so aggressive, so all over the place: managing fifty girls equals managing one boy! But I don't see it negatively. Lord Krishna was like this. He used to create problems in the whole village. Every day the people of the village would complain about him to his mother. She would try to give him a beating, but he would run away and say, "They are all telling lies, I'm such a good boy. They don't like me, so they tell you new stories about me every day. I have never been to their houses. I go to graze my cows." Nevertheless, he was at the centre of all the troubles. He would break the gopi girls' earthen water pots and steal their clothes while they were bathing in the river. When they would request him to return the clothes, he would say, "Come and get them."

Let them play

We have a cricket team for the children of Rikhia. We are organizing a bat and wickets for them, because cricket is the one game which I always liked but did not play. It is a game of calculation, chance and impossibilities. I have never played it, as I had no time to humour myself. I had to work at my schooling and on my property. I was always a busy man. So, all right, if I did not play, let these children play.

These village people do not play tennis or badminton. Those are games of the rich. The poor man's game is football. The game of middle class people and intellectuals is hockey. The game of yogis is cricket. The game of lazy people is golf. In golf, you hit the ball here and remain standing there. You dress smartly, in proper coat and trousers. What kind of game is that if you do not fall, if your clothes do not become dirty, if you do not get tired? What is the use of that game?

You must allow your children to devote as much time to sports as they devote to their studies. I do not know about westerners, but Indians are making a mistake by always insisting on study. In the evening, the mother will insist that the child sits and studies. It seldom happens today that the mother asks the children to go out and play. Is there any mother who tells her children, "Why are you sitting here all the time reading books? Go and play."

There is too much study nowadays. Children have a great deal of nervous energy. Either they use it or there is excess voltage and the brain fuses, just like a bulb. Then the child becomes depressed. His mind goes topsy-turvy and is disturbed. The body has the same kind of energy as you have in electrical cables. The cable fuses at times, and in the same way the mind can also fuse. Physical games are extremely necessary to balance this energy. They are the number one necessity. Purification of the body takes place through sports. During play, the blood circulates through the body many times, and the more the blood circulates, the more it becomes purified.

If a child has a pure brain, then study at school is enough. I do not think children should study at home. This homework business is not good. I do not think any child likes it. If you ask your children, "Do you like homework?" they will say, "No." We also know for a fact that many students who lagged behind in their school studies went on to have brilliant careers. Isaac Newton, who discovered the law of gravity, was a very bad student, the dullest in his class. He became the foremost scientist, and today the law of gravity is the basis of every scientific experiment.

If the child is a dull student, it does not mean that he will remain dull all his life. In my schooldays, I was very bad at mathematics, but ask me any calculation now and I can do it. I do not have to use a calculator. I never got good marks in mathematics. I did not even understand geometry. I do not know why they teach it. It has nothing to do with the brain, with intelligence, with tackling the problems of life, whether in business, family or institutional life.

You have to be able to tackle the problems of your life. If you cannot, then what is the use of being a first-class student? There are many first-class firsts, top ranking boys and girls, who have failed in the domestic environment. They fight, quarrel and get involved in conflicts. Their business is ruined, and they are not able to work. What then is the use of being a first-class first? It is good to have that rank. One gets a medal, one feels happy, but that is only a boost to the ego.

The village children are still slightly submissive. Their society is still suppressed. Even though the children may not like the way their parents think, they still cannot raise their heads. In general, the culture of giving order to children is either finished or moving very fast towards its end. A girl is returning from college in a rickshaw and a boy joins her. They save fifty percent of the fare. If parents begin to scold their children for not following their commands, if the children are forced to obey the parents' commands, they will remain quiet because they have no choice.

I think it is necessary for children to be mischievous. If they are not allowed to be mischievous and are suppressed or restricted, they will become bad later and their parents will not be able to control them. When children are naughty in a small flat, it is very difficult for their parents to handle them due to restricted space, but if there is a property like we have here, who cares? Let the children run five times from one end of the boundary to the other, and then they will be tired and sleep well. For children brought up in apartments it is more difficult. Therefore, the entire culture of people living in flats is different from the culture which you see here. Here in the village environment of Rikhia, children can play, make mischief and exhaust all their energy, and then they sleep well. That kind of mischief is *bala lila,* child's play.

Children have an excess of energy. Therefore, they should run, play and enjoy a lot of sport. It is not good for them to simply sit and study alone. Their energy has to be balanced. Parents have a very bad habit of nagging their children, saying, "You are not studying. Have you done your homework?" Children are never asked, "Why don't you go and play football?" Parents never tell them, "There is a good movie showing today. Take some money and go and see it." In India, when children want to see movies, their parents agree reluctantly. They think their children have the same level of consciousness as they do.

The levels of consciousness of a father and his six-year-old son are entirely different. When the son says, "I want to see a movie," there is a different idea in his mind from when the father who is twenty-eight or thirty wants to see a movie. Their attitude and awareness are different. Children do not have an impure motivation; their level of awareness is very high. Children are very close to God. This is not a stereotyped phrase; it is true that children are pure. The moment we grow up, the distance between God and us widens. We learn a lot of wickedness. This state of innocence is described in the first part of the *Ramacharitamanas*, in which the childhood of Rama is described:

> *While taking food, when the King calls Rama*
> *He does not leave the company of his friends.*
> *When Kaushalya goes to call him,*
> *The Lord struts and runs far away.*
> *The mother runs to catch hold of Him by force,*
> *He, who is not conceivable even by the holy scriptures*
> *Which say that He is unknowable.*
> *Even Lord Shiva is unable to know Him.*
> *At last, when He comes in covered with dust,*
> *The king takes Him in his lap.*
> *Smiling, He takes his food in a hurried manner,*
> *And whenever He finds opportunity,*
> *Runs away with a joyful shout,*
> *His face smeared with curd and rice.*

Games create balance

Children must play and arrangements must be made for this. In my opinion, games or sports should become a subject at school and children should even be given marks for their performance. Games should be compulsory for all children except those who have physical problems. Games, drama and music competitions should go on side by side with intellectual pursuits. What is the use of teaching your child that Akbar was born in 1615 and Aurangzeb in 1750? Who wants to know all this history? I learned so much history, but it is of no use to me. When children have time and want to read, then let them, but do not impose study as a part of their education.

Children do not become great through study or qualifications. They become great through the quality of their mind, intelligence and receptivity. This is based upon how much they are able to receive, retain and give. After all, what were Newton's qualifications? Was he a university graduate? I do not mean that one should not study. One must have qualifications because today this is the system throughout the world and we must respect it. Nevertheless, when children are continually asked, "Have you done your homework?" they become scared of not getting first-class marks in their exams. They worry about what Papa or Mama will say, because if they fail they know they will have to face the music.

The popular notion is that if school children play and have fun, they will fail in their studies and in life. What does it matter if they fail a little in their exams? Parents should tell their children, "Never mind, if you fail you can try again." Of course, parents do not have the courage to say such things. Therefore, their children think, "Other students are fighting for a first division. If I get a second division, what will Daddy say?" This idea, which is drilled into the minds of children, ruins their entire personality. Instead, the child should be told, "Go and study if you like, but do not bother too much about it. It is more important that you play every morning and evening. I am just sending you to school to learn whatever you can. It does not matter if you pass or fail."

I maintain that if they play and have fun alongside their studies, they will be successful; and if they study too much, they will spoil their lives. Playing balances the muscular and nervous energies of children and it circulates blood throughout the system many times over. You should feed your children a rich diet with milk, butter and eggs if you can afford it, and then ask them to run two miles every day. The child who does not run and play, who sits in front of the TV all day or studies with one leg up on the table will develop very sluggish blood circulation, like a choked drain. His studies will suffer and a tutor will need to help him.

If a tutor has to be called to help the child study, it is better that the child is not taught at all! If a mirror is clean, your reflection will be clearly visible, but if you are not able to see your reflection, of what use is the mirror? The power of children to grasp new things is normally so strong that the teacher needs to teach something to them only once. Children listen to a song from the cinema just once and they are able to memorize it, yet they need a tutor to help them learn from the school books. No! Children should be left free to play. I grieve to see what is being done to children these days.

RIKHIA KANYAS

You must remember to rear them (kanyas) to be goddesses. May God bless them so they can learn, read, become educated, dance and sing, and finally earn their own living to take care of their parents too.

We are all very fortunate to be here this pleasant morning. The Sat Chandi Mahayajna 2009 is coming to a point of culmination with the most important aspect of this yajna, worshipping the kanya. The kanyas sitting here epitomize the beauty of Rikhia and the beauty of this yajna. The kanya signifies the aspect of energy when it is raw and also pure, untouched and unaware of its own potential. Through worship, the kanyas become the medium for the descent of the refined and luminous energy of Devi and through them we receive Her blessings. They are good conductors of

the divine energy which we are invoking in this Sat Chandi Mahayajna. They are the channel of the Divine Mother. Just as a copper wire becomes the channel for electrical energy, in the same way the cosmic energy, the divine energy, the Mother, can be apprehended through a medium.

Kanyas represent pure spirit
Man's soul is virgin and the kanya signifies the idea of virginity; that pure spirit which cannot be contaminated. Its pristine beauty and glory cannot be sullied. This year, you will be the guests of that virgin soul, of that virgin reality which represents your inner being, which you do not know and cannot see within you. When you do not know an object, then you have to form a concept. This time the concept is the kanyas of Rikhia. I will introduce you to these beautiful,

innocent children who have been chosen as the medium of the formless, Divine Mother.

In the Shakti tantra, the ultimate reality is conceived as Mother, and certainly the ultimate reality is the mother. The ultimate reality is the mother because progeny begins with the mother. The kanya is the medium of the *shakti*, power, of God. The concept of the kanya is not alien to Christianity. In fact, it is an intrinsic part of it. The Virgin Mary was a kanya.

Replicas of the goddess
This morning we are here to witness the kanya pooja. These kanyas are from Rikhia, all of them. We have kanyas, ex-kanyas, invited kanyas and senior kanyas. These girls are very simple and innocent. Up to the age when they attain puberty they do not know the jugglery of sensual life. There are many who, even after puberty, remain virgins mentally and spiritually. Once puberty approaches, the whole system changes within the body, within the structure and psychology of the mind, in the emotional actions and reactions.

Kanya worship is a most important part of Shakti tantra. I have been waiting for this moment. I feel very happy and I want you also to feel very happy, because you are being presented with a new concept, you are being initiated into a new philosophy of life where a little girl can be the replica of the goddess. The concept of the kanya is unparalleled in man's philosophy. The discovery that a young virgin was capable of symbolizing and representing the Cosmic Mother was made by a rishi. Could you ever think of your little daughter as the replica of the Mother? No. The idea did not come to the people, only to those rishis, the great seers who saw very clearly.

Just as you see greed in money, passion in a woman, fear in a ghost or tiger, similarly why can't you see the goddess in the kanyas? Why do you need to be convinced? Why should I convince you? It is your daily experience that where there is money, there is greed. Money represents greed. The replica of greed is money. The replica of passion is a woman. The replica of fear is a tiger. The replicas of the goddess are here. You do not have to prove it. It is as simple as that!

For the last twenty years, the kanya pooja has been going on here. Many of those kanyas have now left Rikhia. In the course of time, the children you see here now will also go out. All these children are intrinsically related to the ashram. The whole morning they are in the school which is next to the ashram. Thereafter, they are in the ashram. They only go back to their cottages or dwelling at night, at six or seven o'clock, and as soon as it is morning they get out. They are always with the ashram and in the ashram. So we will say they are ashram kanyas.

Kanyas are the host

All of you are the guests of this grand Sat Chandi Mahayajna, and these kanyas are your hosts. The priest will be a kanya, the caterer will be a kanya, the singer will be a kanya, and the controller of every ritual of this yajna will be a kanya.

These kanyas do not belong to the upper crust of society, what is called the 'creamy layer'. They do not even belong to the middle class or the lower middle class of society. They belong to the strata of society which many in the West, and even in India, do not know about. It is called 'no class'. They have no status in society. They collect cow dung every morning. They carry the load and stock of paddy and wheat from the field to the granary. They take the cattle for grazing. They rise early before sunrise and go out in the fields for their toilet. They bathe in the pond and then they walk great distances to collect dried leaves to take home so their mother can light a fire to cook the family's food. They have a very different way of life, which you cannot even imagine, but at this yajna you will be their guests.

This is a very sacred tantric ceremony in which the kanyas are worshipped as the living, breathing manifestation of Devi. They are not Devi, they are the medium of Devi, through whom she will manifest and bless us all.

SRI SWAMIJI'S LAST DARSHAN
2nd December 2009, Yoga Poornima, Rikhiapeeth

The kanyas of Rikhia have successfully organized two yajnas. The first one was Sat Chandi Mahayajna, the second one is Mahamrityunjaya Yajna. Both these yajnas were successfully managed by the kanyas and batuks of Rikhia. You have all been a witness to this. Rikhia is not like Chennai, Mumbai, Kolkata or Delhi; it is a very small village where I came twenty years ago. These children had not even been born then. Twenty years ago, at twelve noon on 23rd September, 1989 I set up my tent in the adjoining property. None of the old men from that era survive today, maybe only a handful.

The feeling and attitude that has germinated in these children is one of sadhana and yoga. If you cannot see and appreciate the dexterity, perseverance and selflessness with which these children have conducted the two yajnas, what can I do?

All our sannyasins sit over there. No one ever need get up. I don't even come here. Swami Niranjan just stands around. And Swami Satsangi just chitchats with you people. Food is cooked for tens of thousands of people, the serving of meals continues, the distribution of prasad continues, the kirtan-bhajan continues. And these children don't just sing simple school prayers. They sing the classical prayers chanted in the monasteries of sannyasins, in the ashrams of jagadgurus. They chant the prayers, mantras and hymns sung in the assemblies of learned pandits and saints.

This means that there is genuine potential hidden within these children. There are hundreds of thousands of such villages together with such children throughout India. They are the future of this country, but there is no one to look after them. Their fathers drink, smoke, gamble, steal and womanize. They don't care for their children. These children have been born by accident. Today, all of you are gathered here, so I won't mince words.

Message to Rikhia panchayat

The duty of parents is to live like sannyasins and raise their children properly. These children are your future. After marriage, these girls will go to another home. Not as mere brides, but as ambassadors. They are ambassadors of refined culture. Whatever good or bad they've learnt here in the ashram they will take with them to their new homes.

I know how careless and irresponsible you parents are. Drinking liquor in the middle of the night! If drinking and gambling was all you wanted to do, why did you marry and beget children in the first place? You should have just stayed with the prostitutes you visit. You have ruined the life of a woman, a child, this society and this nation.

Children should be given the right samskaras. Until they can realize their potential, until proper arrangements are made for their food, clothing, recreation and education, your future can never be bright. You will never receive the grace of Lakshmi, the goddess of prosperity. After all, what will Lakshmi do in your house? You don't even have a proper toilet or bed to offer her!

Rectify your life from today itself. Today is Margasheersha Poornima. Margasheersha is considered the best among months and today is the best poornima. Let go of all your vices and bad habits in the name of your children. Make a solemn resolve that you will not indulge in those vices again. And that you will never beat your wife again.

Just a few days ago, the daughter of a well-to-do family got married here. A kanya asked her, "What will you do if your husband beats you?" She replied, "Beats me? Does he have the guts to do that?!"

Today, when you go back to your homes, ponder over what I have said. Visiting the temple and drinking liquor right after does not please God; for God is not pleased by such empty rituals. You will have to change your entire outlook on life. Today the whole of Rikhia is gathered here, which is why I am saying these things. I am not lecturing on religion, just talking about your own good. This was the first point.

The second point is that we will teach yoga to these children. The necessary arrangements will soon be made. A huge hall is ready in Rikhia, we will teach yoga there. By 'yoga', I mean asana and pranayama. Through the practice of asana and pranayama, the children will stay healthy and fit, their minds will become alert and sharp, and they will be able to think and decide about their own future. Not to mention beautiful, shining faces! The kanyas who were just dancing looked beautiful, didn't they?

We will teach yoga to the children. But then don't start complaining that "Through yoga Swamiji will make the children sannyasins." In fact, if I could do that, that would be the best thing for you. You wouldn't have to worry about your daughters' marriage or dowry. They would stay for free in the ashram. I would feed all of them. Why? Because they are my daughters. You have begotten them by accident. In reality they belong to me. Tell me, who gives all of you new clothes five-six times a year, your father or me?

Kanya-batuks: You!

And who is arranging for your daily meals here in the ashram, your father or me?

Kanya-batuks: You!

Who is giving all the books and notebooks for your schooling? Your father or me?

Kanya-batuks: You!

Did you hear your children's answer? Therefore, deal with them in a proper manner from now on. Don't slap them. These kids eat all the guavas and mangoes from our trees. But I have told everyone in the ashram, don't even dare touch these children. If a child makes mischief, think that Kanhaiya has incarnated in your home! If children cannot be mischievous, who can? You? If you are mischievous, the police will catch you and you will go straight to jail. Let the children be naughty. After all, what harm can they do?

Let me tell you about Swami Niranjan himself. Once when he was six years old, he opened up my tape recorder. In those days, a tape recorder used to be a luxury. When I asked him why he had opened it up, he replied that he was trying to learn the tape recorder's mechanism! Now what should have I done? Slapped him? Would that have repaired my tape recorder? No, but it would have definitely damaged his tape recorder.

Never ever hit these children or abuse them, otherwise their tape recorder will get damaged and the harmony of your entire family will be shattered. So, stop beating your children, and always remember that they are the embodiments of love.

Namo Narayan

WOMEN

Debt to my mother

Let me tell you the background first. Whatever I am doing here in Rikhia is in repayment of the debt I owe to a woman, my mother. A sannyasin owes his mother the biggest debt. Adi Shankaracharya had to discontinue his world-conquering tour to discharge his duty towards his mother by performing her last rites when she died. All other debts recorded in the register of Chitragupta can be written off except that owed to one's mother.

As a sannyasin and as a man I am indebted to my mother. When I talk like this I represent all men. We are all indebted to our mothers. I am indebted to my mother who gave me the secrets of success in life, who guided me and put me on the right path, from whom I imbibed all the good samskaras that percolate through the pores of my body and the whole of my being, and who also let me go and leave home in search of God. You may write off any other debt in this world except the debt to your mother. Even God, Lord Rama, had to discharge the debt towards his mother when he incarnated as a human being. Mother is the life giver, the jnana giver, the samskara giver. She shapes the destiny of her child.

Just as the future of a tree is embedded in the seed, the destiny of a child is imprinted in the womb of the mother. If the seed is faulty, the tree cannot be strong. You may make liberal use of pesticides and fertilizers, but it will prove futile. It is essential that the mother, the nourisher and procreator, is beautiful. It matters little whether she is an ordinary woman or an extraordinary woman.

Today, at the age of seventy-five, I hold my mother exclusively responsible for everything I have achieved and lost in my life so far, for everything that I have thought and done. Therefore, my first priority is to repay my mother. Now what can be done to clear this debt? In India, the majority of women are exploited and downtrodden. Maybe 0.01 percent of women are the exception. An ordinary woman has no means of education, advancement or legal protection, and it is we who have deprived her of all these things. Therefore, I proclaim it as the duty of each and every sannyasin to help and support these women.

I am not a great man. I am a small man living in a small place, so I decided to begin in a small way. Even if I can bring about the upliftment of a limited number of girls, my life will have become worthwhile and I will be satisfied. I do not think I am responsible for all the women of India or Asia, therefore I decided to undertake Sita Kalyanam within the confines of my neighbourhood, Rikhia panchayat. If a sadhu does not support the woman deprived of everything, who else will? This is of primary importance to the spiritual aspect of woman as mother. People say that sadhus and sannyasins should have nothing to do with the female sex; and that they should not even talk to women. I say, "Why not?" You must remember that the race, the tradition, the people who do nothing to uplift their downtrodden womenfolk can never rise. No society can progress without giving their dues to women. Even India will never enjoy prosperity until it makes its womenfolk stand on their own two feet, makes them great and learned.

Here in Rikhia we try to help and promote the women, and I am already famous or infamous for that. However, I don't mind what people say, because if saints and sages do not fulfil their duty towards women, then who will? Most people are afraid to be outspoken, but what have I to fear? I do not care about or pay any attention to whatever slander and abuse is spread against me. I let it go in one ear and out the other. Don't we have a duty and an obligation towards women? We have been closest to a woman because we have lived in her womb for nine months. We emerged into this world out of her body, so why should we feel different from her? Why should we try to separate ourselves from her? When God has not done this, why should we?

Symbols of my mother

Years ago I realized that all the women in the world, including young girls, are my mothers. All women represent your mother, whether eastern or western, modern or traditional, young or old, companion or secretary, urban dweller or villager. I have not forgotten this even for a moment. A woman comes into your life as a mother, as a daughter. The strongest manifestation of God in this world is the woman as mother. She is the best of His beauty, the best representation of His benediction and grace. Therefore, as a sannyasin I am freeing myself from the debt to my mother.

I do not care what people say, it is my right to respect women, to love women, to protect women and to give them everything that I have to give. I will give whatever I can to women. I can give love, respect and equality, and these things must be given to women. This is our dharma, duty and obligation because we are their children.

A woman's nature is always that of a mother. Whether a woman is your wife or daughter, her nature is that of a mother, and the mother too was a woman once. My mother was also a woman and I am very thankful to her for producing me. The qualities which I have imbibed are not due to my father. The credit for creating my life goes to my mother, not to my father, because he was only a medium.

In tune with the times

A woman is a precious gem; she is a pearl, a diamond. You should have realized her value, yet such a worthy part of society is reduced to a nonentity. This is their helpless state, especially in villages; they have been exploited, ill-treated, dishonoured and weakened. Women cannot go to school and cannot mix freely in society, cannot take a lift from a boy on their way to college.

It is time for women to learn to think differently. To begin with, a woman should stop thinking like a servant. She is the master of the house and she must think like that. Times are changing very rapidly and she must think accordingly. Today girls wear jeans, before that they wore miniskirts and before that full Victorian dresses. Here in my village, the uneducated Santhali girls who work as labourers told Swami Satsangi, "We want to wear jeans because we have difficulty working in petticoats and saris." So we gave them all jeans and now the girls who come to work as labourers wear jeans and caps.

Valuable female qualities

Women have much more forbearance and fortitude, what is called *nigraha shakti*, than men. Men often let go of their principles, but women have more restraint. Women have a greater capacity to bear pain and endure hardship than men. If men had to give birth to a child, they would surely die. Just imagine how much pain a woman goes through while giving birth to a child! The pain at the time of delivery is the pain of death.

There is another amazing thing that they do. They can go into a stranger's house and make it their own; they become the *maharanis* of that place. They become the Lakshmi of the house. Is that an ordinary quality? Do men go to their wives' parental homes? The man who stays at his wife's parental home has no personality remaining. He suffers from a sense of inferiority, but women can go to their in-laws and remain superior! Women have a basic ability to adjust in this manner.

They do not say, "I am going to my husband's house." They say, "I am going to my father-in-law's house."

The other quality that women have is *viveka*, discrimination between right and wrong, the ability to distinguish between *dharma* and *adharma*. If a man was required to go out to work and keep the house and take care of the children, he would go insane. But the women go to work, give birth to children, feed them, keep house, go to the market and do other things as well. A man will go ahead and drink Scotch even if he does not have money to pay his bills, but a woman will never do this.

It is important that we have a special respect, regard and recognition for the women of our homes, the wife, mother, daughter, daughter-in-law or sister. We must change

our attitude towards women completely and have greater faith in their purity and willpower. Women have *sankalpa shakti,* willpower. Once they decide something, they do it. Therefore, in this context, women have superior qualities, not only in India, but the world over. You can verify this anywhere in the world. The traits of women remain the same. Women have valuable qualities. We will have to acknowledge, value and respect them, and utilize these qualities for building the nation as well as the family.

Special needs
I try to help the girls of this region through education. Sita Kalyanam is also organized for this purpose. I have observed that girls have a special fondness for certain things in life. First and foremost, the girl who wants to survive and make headway needs stability and security. This is a female's inborn nature. Women have no ambition except to become stable. Stability is their weakness as well as their quality. A woman will try to become stable wherever she goes, whether it is at her in-laws, in an office or in an ashram. A stable person whose mind and body are focused is needed to manage any institution.

Today, if men try to run the household, they will fail because they are not good managers. Let them try to look after the kitchen, the children, the cleaning, as well as the maintenance, and everything will collapse. In the evening, instead of sugar there will be salt in the tea! Therefore, in the coming age, the women of India must become Mother India, and it is our duty to see that this happens. Leave aside old ideas that men and women become impure if they touch each other. The touch of a woman, whether a mother, lover or wife, purifies and sanctifies a man. Similarly, the touch of a man makes a woman powerful. A woman touching a man and man touching a woman, both are important and have their place.

I want to help the women who want to preserve their femininity instead of imitating the rough and tough ways of the male. Wherever she goes, I want her to be the ruler and the queen. Thirdly, women are fond of wearing jewellery and ornaments to beautify themselves. When you present a sari, a diamond ring or even just a small ornament to a girl or a woman, she is always very pleased. This is her characteristic feature. Therefore, I will give her all the three things here and receive the cooperation of all and sundry. I have started helping women out by giving them bicycles and inspiration, and with God's grace I will continue to do so. Each girl will be the symbol of my mother.

Equal rights for women
We give bicycles to those girls who go to school in Deoghar. I help the girls because we have to atone for all the oppression heaped upon girls and women in the past. This is an obligation we have to fulfil. Women have been tortured and are being humiliated even today in India. Their rights and privileges have been snatched away. Many degrading rules have been imposed on them. All the facilities and privileges centre only on men. Women and girls are ordered not to do this and not to do that. India and Indians have to atone for the heartless acts and atrocities committed towards women.

In ancient India, in the vedic culture, women also used to receive the sacred thread, the *yajnopaveeta*, and they practised japa of the Gayatri mantra. They also used to practise sandhya vandana, but later on India became a prey to foreign invaders. Many cultures, ideas, races and philosophies came in, and when these became politically powerful, they imposed their systems on the society. Degradation of women is alien to vedic culture where women were in the forefront of society. They were made to recede into the background because of frequent invasions.

Vedic culture was different. At that time, women had a prime place in society. All the systems were named after women. Vedic culture never talks of *pitrivansha*, but of *matrivansha*, maternal lineage. It never talks of *pitribhoomi*, but of *matribhoomi*, motherland. The names of male offspring were given according to the names of their mothers: Kaushalyanandan, Rama; Kaunteya, Pandavas; and Devakinandan, Krishna. The same patriarchal dominance, however, happens in every nation when a foreign culture comes in. Gradually, they take political power, attain economic power and thus get a hold over the society and the people have to accept what they say.

In vedic culture, women sat in parliament. Gargi was in the court of Janaka, the King of Videha. If you read the *Brihadaranyaka Upanishad*, you will find that Gargi asked Yajnavalkya, in court, to define the imperishable government. He replied, "I will explain it to you. The imperishable government is the one with the eternal law. The law of the movement of heavenly bodies is the imperishable government. By this law, the sun and the moon move in their respective directions and their movements can be calculated thousands of years before they start moving." There are records of many such exchanges.

Over the last few years in India things have been changing and women are again coming out because of the balancing effect of modern culture. It is pleasing to see women as a part of our society and not merely a part of the kitchen, toilet or laundry.

Encourage strength and confidence
Now in Rikhia we have employment plans for all the women, including carpentry, electrical work and farm work with the newest methods. There will be work for old women and education for little girls. There should be some art and attainment possible for women and girls, something for poor working women and girls too, and then the bidi making will come to an end here. In a few decades, they will be very active in this society. That is the contribution and the influence of the modern West with their growing respect for women.

The truth is that men and women must have equal rights. The rules governing both must be the same. The civil and social laws must be similar; they cannot and should not be unequal and different. The same laws should apply to both men and women. Why can't a girl go somewhere alone like a boy does? Only because some of the boys may get up to mischief with her. If a girl is made stronger and more confident from the very beginning, then if anyone tries to misbehave with her she will be able to fully defend herself. Girls should be allowed to grow strong from early childhood and must not be kept under restraint.

In England, only one hundred and fifty years ago, women were not allowed into the office. The first woman secretary employed in an office went to work every day with her body completely covered from top to bottom. She was placed in a separate room with a little table outside, on which she would place the completed typewritten papers. These would then be collected. So, western society was equally backward, but modern culture has begun to revolutionize these ancient concepts.

From childhood I have been obsessed by their plight, because within our society women are a helpless lot, and I don't like this situation. I feel that women must be allowed to live as freely as men, and I have always spoken openly about it. I have given women the maximum possible patronage, even in the institutional affairs of ashram life. Although not everybody responded well to this idea, I did not care and gave women every possible opportunity. Even today, I always tell the villagers that women should be allowed to live as freely as men. This seems to be my karma. I have realized it, so what do I do? I've made it clear that all the girls in my neighbourhood must be helped through education and marriage. Of course, if they want to take sannyasa, well and good, but not everybody should take sannyasa.

Until everyone in India is provided education, until everyone can stand on their own feet, until the social, political, legal and constitutional structure with regard to women changes, the problems of the country will not be solved. In India, fifty percent of women are completely illiterate and victims of superstition. Their men keep them safe, provide food and clothing, so they can subsist; they cannot subsist on their own. Some of the young women

working here as labourers know nothing about pregnancy or labour pain. Half of India's population is not capable of self-reliance. What can you expect from a society whose population is so weak, so lame that it cannot walk without help from others? This is a matter of great disappointment.

Since I have been here in Rikhia the percentage of girls registering in the schools has increased. I have not asked them to go to school, but they see the female sannyasins full of confidence and courage driving cars, trucks and tractors, supervising construction work and going to the market. So they have imbibed this desire to learn and to become something. I have only one principle: to make good quality products, you need good quality machines. A sub-standard machine can only produce a sub-standard product.

Everyone knows that a female gives birth to another human being which grows and derives nourishment inside her body. These young girls are the manufacturing machines of the future. Males are only the operators. After all, we are all born from the womb of a female. Whatever the mother's internal condition may be, whether nectar or poison, this will directly affect the child. He will inherit her weaknesses and diseases as well as her strengths and intellect. In science this is called 'genetic transfer'. We are the genetic transfer of our parents. Therefore, females should exercise at all ages of their life. For this reason, girls should play, for they will bear the children of the next generation.

There are many games, like skipping, which provide very good exercise. There are a few games which are not meant for girls, but they should certainly join in other games and sports, keeping in mind their physical nature. Asanas have their own importance, but women should also go for walks and outings. Social restrictions on females, such as staying indoors behind curtained windows and not appearing before men, no longer apply in modern society. Now that society has permitted women so much freedom, they should use it for their benefit. So, whether the product is good or bad depends on them. Therefore, we must educate, encourage and inspire girls to create a dynamic community, not a passive one.

Treasurers of society
In the villages, the men can never exploit the women because, in India, the woman is *grihalakshmi*, the ruler of the house. She is like the home minister, and in many countries the home minister is more powerful than the prime minister. It is she who controls the family wealth, the gold, silver and jewellery.

In case you do not know, I will explain the most important point. In India, there is a very ancient law that has survived for thousands of years. A man cannot touch, sell or transfer the wealth that belongs to a woman, no matter whether she is his wife, mother or sister. The wealth that belongs to her will go to her daughters or daughters-in-law, but not to her husband or son. That is called *streedhanam*. The word *stree* means wife, and *dhanam* means wealth. If the husband compels his wife to give him her wealth, whatever it is, whether property, a car, ornaments, gold, silver or pearls, she can sue him in a court of law. The court will say, "No,

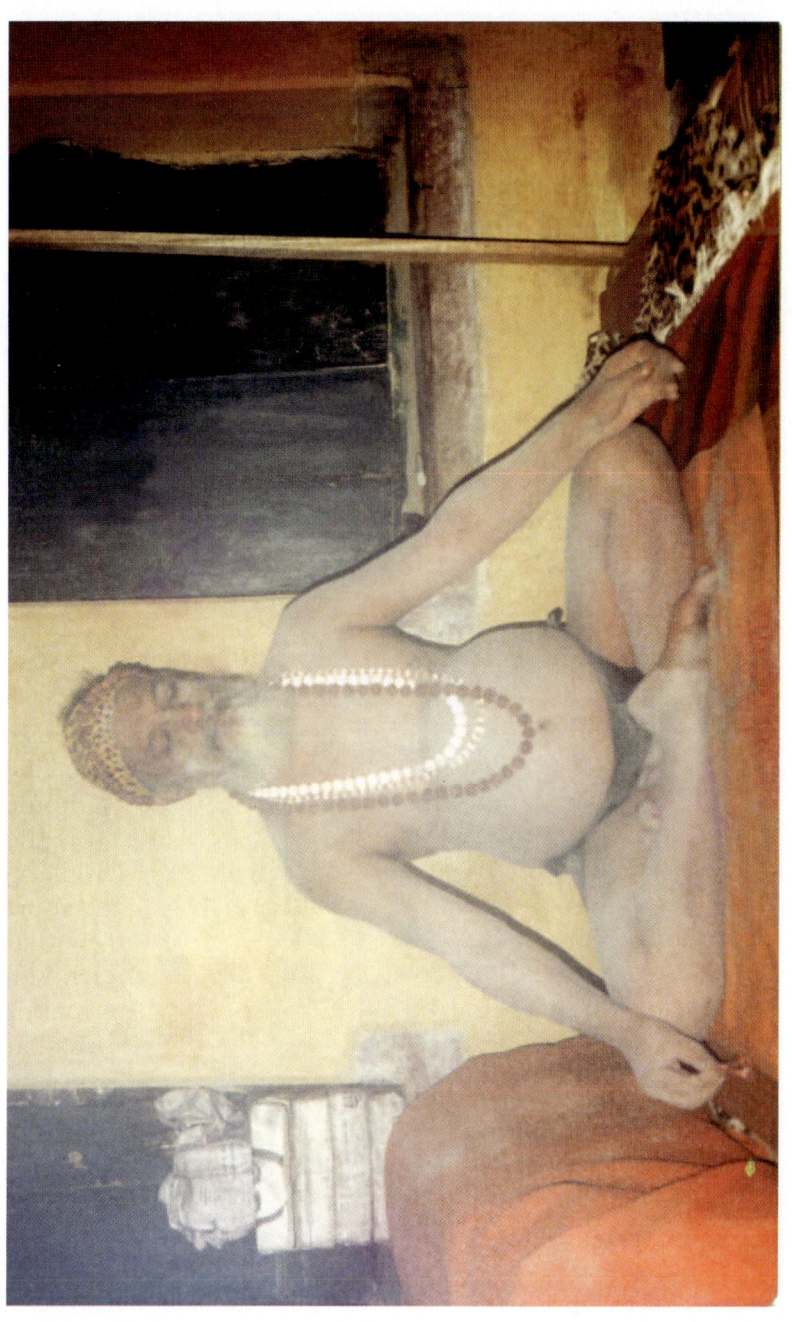

he cannot touch it; this is her property." The property and rights of women are completely protected by law.

The husbands of these poor labouring women you see in the villages do not know where their wives keep the ornaments. In Indian villages, the family home has only one room, fifteen-by-fifteen or ten-by-ten, but the husband does not know where the gold is hidden. The wife goes out daily to till the land or to labour somewhere because she is from a very poor family. However, her mother-in-law remains at home all day, like a watchdog; she never goes out. Therefore, the mother-in-law has a very secure place in the family, as the daughter-in-law needs her to look after the wealth, the ornaments and jewels, in her absence, so that the husband does not dig them up and run away.

In rural areas, the mother-in-law and daughter-in-law get on very well, which is not the case in urban society. If the husband is given to drinking or womanizing, he could dig up the whole room while the wife goes out to work. He would easily find out where the wealth is kept and run away with it, but for the mother-in-law who is there all the time on guard, like an Alsatian. This is the secret of our society, which is called streedhanam. So, in India, there are two types of wealth: national and personal. Every family will have at least ten to one hundred grams of gold. Those families which are better off will have from one to ten kilograms, and some families may have fifteen to twenty kilograms of gold.

The government does not know and cannot know about this wealth. If the government encroaches upon women's personal wealth, it will fall. It will not come to power next time. No government and no man can touch a woman's wealth. She is the sole administrator. In 1962, there was an Indo-Chinese conflict. Indian and Chinese military forces gathered on the borders. At that time of national crisis, women came forward with large numbers of personal gold bangles, earrings and nose-rings, which they gave to the government. They said, "Go and fight and protect our borders." Therefore, never misunderstand the power, posi-

tion and capacity of an Indian woman. If the woman is such a powerful person in society, she has to be looked after. Their nature is to be secure, stable and to rule.

I am giving these good luck kits, to these daughters-in-law, my daughters-in-law, your daughters-in-law, with ornaments, jewels and nice things, not because I want to make the family rich by giving them, but to help nurture and sustain society for times to come. A few days ago, a girl of fifteen was leaving and I asked her, "If I were to give you something, what would you choose?" She replied, "Something made out of gold." That girl was so poor that her clothes were in tatters. Her family had not eaten for days, and she was dreaming of gold! Here the women dream of gold, and why not? For they are the treasurers of society. If you want to help a nation, a culture or humanity, make sure that you look after womankind.

Birthplace of the new Devi
The village women sing beautifully while they work. We used to have them over to grind grain. They would sing while grinding, and I encouraged them to continue. Apart

from a few, most village women are totally illiterate, but they know all the dates, festivals, nakshatras, and phases of the moon. They remember the entire yearly calendar of events. They know when it is Panchami, Chhat or Teej. The educated do not know all this; they have to ask the pandit when it is Ekadashi. These women have maintained these old traditions. Had it not been for them, our traditions would have been lost.

Women are the central pivot of a family. If she is inspired, her family will follow suit. If the woman of the family wakes up, the entire family awakens. If the woman sleeps, whether the mother, wife or daughter, the entire family sleeps. It is the duty of men to pay as much attention to their daughters as to their sons. Women are one foot of society and men the other. If one foot is strong and the other is weak, the society will be lame. Tell me, isn't this a lame society at the moment?

With my encouragement, many women will begin to read *Ramacharitamanas*. I have told them from the very beginning to read this scripture or *Hanuman Chalisa*. Normally, I do not meet them. It is only for the last four or five days that the censorship laws between them and me have become lenient. I will see them for another month and then take one year's leave. Meanwhile, I will continue to inspire them to undertake these projects.

Simplicity and stability

Right now, these women are employed in the home and they know how to run the family well and to lead a very harmonious and healthy life. They are not in league with the unemployed of India. For most Indian village women, the day begins with a bath and worship of *tulsi*, holy basil plant. Since they do not have toilets at home, they go out of the village. Then they go to the water tank where they bathe and wash their clothes. After that, they pick flowers from the garden, go to the temple, do their pooja, come home and worship tulsi. Then they worship their *kula devata*, family deity, and sit down for breakfast. The women do all this early in the morning for an hour, and then the day begins. Prior to that, the husbands have to do everything for themselves. They cannot say, "Get me my tea."

I am talking about illiterate women as well as educated women who live here in Rikhia. We have many educated women, and they are very devoted to spiritual life. This is the influence which their children imbibe. If the child goes wrong, it is a problem for the mother. Whenever a child errs, it is neither the fault of the son, the daughter or society. The blame lies entirely with the mother. You may like it or dislike it, which is up to you to decide, but I must tell you the truth. Mothers in India cannot bear this. It is a big blow to the mother, because she thinks it is due to her sins. She feels it is her fault which is being projected in the child's life, because the child belongs to the mother. Socially and legally, he may belong to the father, but naturally he belongs to the mother. Children belong ninety-nine percent to women and one percent to men. Therefore, in India, they will ask which is your mother's place. They will say motherland, not fatherland, and mother tongue, not father tongue. We know that it is politics, the legal system, international and cultural influences, which have made Indian society patriarchal. We accept it, but there is no doubt that the basis of Indian family life is matriarchal.

Honour the Lakshmi

Women are the main asset in the Indian family. When the wife comes to her husband's home, she does not come empty-handed; however, he goes to her house like a beggar to fetch her. It is she who manages all the expenses of the marriage. She comes to his house with a full set of pots, suitcases, a cycle, a rickshaw, a scooter, a car, a TV, a video set, an audio set, jewellery, and also a minimum of sixty to seventy thousand rupees in cash. She comes as Lakshmi, the goddess of wealth, and he keeps her there as his servant. Even her son will not clean the pots and utensils. Her children leave their plates on the table after eating, so that she, the mother,

will clean up. The VIP who came to her husband's house and filled it with wealth is today the maidservant. This is the biggest mistake of Indian society; it is like ploughing a field with an elephant or killing a mosquito with a cannon. People will have to rethink.

I feel kindness for and also affinity with the mother, daya and maya both. In my heart there is a big place for the mother, the beautiful creation of God. I have been a supporter of women and girls for many years. Many people have also said, "Sri Swamiji keeps girls with him." Well, if not girls, then who shall I keep? Man wants to keep beautiful flowers with him, not thorns. No one keeps thorns in the house. My ashram thrived because I trained females and gave them responsible posts. Women are very sincere. They do not have the habit of smoking, drinking, gambling or going to the cinema. The administration of the Bihar School of Yoga was never in my hands because I was mostly out travelling. I never saw the chequebooks, passbooks, registers or accounts. Here, Swami Satsangi manages everything. It is not that the male swamis are redundant, each one has his place; however, now I am talking about women.

When Swami Satsangi first came to Rikhia, she was completely ignorant of rural India and rural life. She comes from that generation in India where girls prefer to 'snack and dance', to put on a Michael Jackson CD. She knew all about that culture. She had no idea about rural culture, but since she was living here with me, naturally she had to attune herself to these surroundings. Swami Satsangi was so ignorant of rural life that she did not know the difference between a cow and a bull! She did not know how the people in rural India lived. In the first few years she worked very hard building and learning about rural life. Then Bihar School of Yoga and Sivananda Math came forward to assist her. Now she knows everything, the ABCD of everything, totally. She has become an asset for the people here and they like her. She inspires confidence in the village girls.

At the same time, however, she has a very strong personality. She gives it to everyone left, right and centre. There is no question of formality and talks. She calls a rose a rose and a spade a spade. A person who shoulders responsibility should be very strong. Of course, after me she will carry on the work of Sivananda Math very well. I do not deal with the management, planning or administration of this place at all. Initially I used to tell her what to do, but not now.

Make them Chandi

The people of our country must understand one fact. The fall of India is entirely because the left half remains weak and ineffective. The female side is paralyzed and has developed debility. What do our women do? They pick up cow dung, sweep and wash. They bear children and get beaten. What do our men do? They chew betel leaf, drink, chase other women, disappear from home night after night, then visit the temple and worship Kali and Durga. Bravo for the men!

A woman is shakti, energy, power, but today if someone teases her on the road, she can't do anything. No boy is afraid of her. When she tries to defend herself with her sandals or bag, it doesn't put him off. Therefore, girls should learn some skills for self-protection, like karate, so if any male misbehaves with them on the road they can just give him a kick and reorganize his skeletal structure. Then no boy will dare to look at a girl with bad intentions. Girls are not weak and defenceless by nature; it is the male who has made them that way in order to exploit them. A person who is weak can always be exploited, but not one who is strong.

If a girl becomes strong then no one will be able to exploit her. Before a man can even open his mouth, she will have told him to shut up. Here in the villages, the man drinks toddy, gets drunk, comes home and beats up his wife. The woman, who has brought ten to twenty thousand rupees, a cycle, saris, suits, a scooter, audio equipment and so on, is bashed up by her husband. This is a shameful act. The screws are loose in the husband's head and the wife does not know how to tighten them up.

When the husband has a strong wife he cannot drink alcohol, smoke cigarettes or have illicit relationships with other women, because a strong wife will never allow it. She will tell him, "If you want to live properly then do so, otherwise get out and don't come back." A woman must have such authority, such power, such rights, so that she can pull the man's ears and also keep a tight control on the keys.

Everybody has to dedicate themselves to the task of uplifting women, of helping them on the path of progress. Let society condemn and criticize you for this. Somebody has to bell the cat, so I am that rat who is belling the cat.

Deoghar is the cremation ground of Sati. Lord Shiva roamed around the whole world, mad with despair at the death of his consort Sati, carrying her dead body on his shoulders. During the journey the different parts of her body fell in different regions. The last part remaining on his shoulder was her heart, which fell here. Therefore, this is the seat of Devi's heart. This is not the cremation ground of Shiva, but of Sati, and it is also the birthplace of the new Devi. The message for the awakening of the woman will go out from here. Therefore, give a proper education to the women in your house, to your daughters, mothers and sisters, and make them Chandi.

RIKHIA WIDOWS

Last year He said to me, "There are many helpless widows in your neighbourhood. What have you thought of for them?" I said, "What can I think of? You tell me and I will carry it out."

When the social status of women was very low in India, a widowed woman was totally alone and unprotected once her husband died. She was in a constant state of anxiety about her fate as a widow. She was forced to discard her jewellery, to break her bangles and throw away her necklace. Sometimes she was forced to climb on her husband's pyre and accept self-immolation. All these ghastly compulsions made her unstable and she would go insane. Such an unsteady, unbalanced and oppressed person could not be entrusted to perform the last rites. Such a deranged woman was capable of throwing herself into the fire while performing the rites. Surely our modern society cannot impose unreasonable restraints on widows.

Widows cannot even wear a ring! Widows are forced to shave their heads. Why aren't widowers also compelled to do that? Many people force widows to wear white clothes. Does a widower wear the same? No. All these rules of society are for women only. So, I directed that all the widows of this panchayat should be offered coloured saris and clothes similar to those of married women. We follow the normal practice and you will not be able to distinguish a widow from a married woman on the basis of their clothing. Why are widows directed not to wear good clothes and ornaments? I cannot appreciate the restrictive social customs of the widow and widower and this rite will not hold good here in Rikhia panchayat. My mind does not accept it.

Recently, the villagers of Rikhia decided upon a consensus that widows should be permitted to remarry. I told them, "You all sit and put your heads together in the panchayat and decide. Those who do not want to marry should not be forced to do so, but those who need to or wish to remarry should be remarried." Notes like this are exchanged between the villagers and me. Those widows who do not want to remarry should be left alone. It is a good thing if they want to remain alone: *Alakh Niranjan*, but there are many other factors involved in the widow remarriage issue, like economic and emotional problems. Widow remarriage has now become the norm in all the villages here. The government formulates laws, but what can laws do to bring about change?

Auspicious employment

Here in Rikhia God has given me two directions: "Love your neighbours as I have loved you" and "Help your neighbours as I have helped you." These are His orders and He will also implement them. Last year He said to me, "There are many helpless widows in your neighbourhood. What have you thought of for them?" I said, "What can I think of? You tell me and I will carry it out."

So, in the coming year, from Makar Sankranti, I will have the poor widows seated in the hall in which you were singing kirtan this morning. We have built a home for the widows. It is called Tapovanam because widows are also a kind of *tapasvini* or ascetic. Our greatest tapasvinis have been widows. Who is better at austerities than they? Those women who become widows are asked to give up coloured clothes and are permitted to wear only white. They are not supposed to wear jewellery of gold or silver. They are banned from auspicious ceremonies and weddings. They are not allowed to meet men. You people have laid down many rules for widows in the name of the shastras. I cannot break these rules; neither did I want to, because it is your society and social code, not mine. But here, they will be given wages for their daily labour of chanting, writing and reading God's name; and here, every year, they are my special guests at the Sat Chandi Mahayajna.

I will tell the illiterate ones to chant the Maha Mantra for eight hours and then give them wages at the end of the day for their day's work of chanting. This year we have made a budget for one hundred widows. Those who are literate will be given a notebook in which to write the name of *Rama* until the end of the day. I will collect all those notebooks and keep them. Whenever you plan to build a house, you can take a few of them from me and put them in the foundations. Those widows who are educated will be given the *Ramacharitamanas* to read. They will be given a separate room in which there will be a picture of Lord Rama. There will be provision for all three classes of widows: illiterate, literate and educated.

THE ELDERLY

Employed in God's name

I have made a program for the elderly people of Rikhia and the surrounding areas. It is a very unusual program. All the old folk who can neither work at home nor earn wages by working outside will be called here and given a payment. There will be double wages for them. They will earn in the name of *Rama* and for repeating His name they will be given remuneration in the form of money. I am planning to build a hall in this enclosure where you are all sitting. Needy men and women will come here at eight o'clock in the morning and will be asked to do japa of the Lord until four o'clock in the evening. At the end of the day they will be paid for their labour of love.

The rate of payment will be the same as the government gives to daily wage earners. The only difference is that young people get paid for hard manual work, like carrying heavy stones, working with spades, mixing cement and building materials, cutting steel, driving taxis and trekkers. These old people cannot do such heavy work, so they will get paid for a different type of work. Old people are considered good for nothing. The whole day they sit at home and get abused. We will engage them here from 8 am to 4 pm. I will work out a way to prevent any shirking, because it is a widespread habit to dodge work. Even in matters relating to God, people will try to avoid work.

At first, I will have a group of about twenty to twenty-five people and afterwards I will call more. This will be a novel plan of employment. I am facing the problem now of how to give employment to the villagers. At first I had houses built, one after another, but that is not a good idea. I do not want to set up an ashram here. Whatever I have done is already more than enough, but if I could give them employment then their unemployment problem would be solved. These days, people create old-age homes, but that is a futile venture. I have seen it to be a failure, even in modern countries.

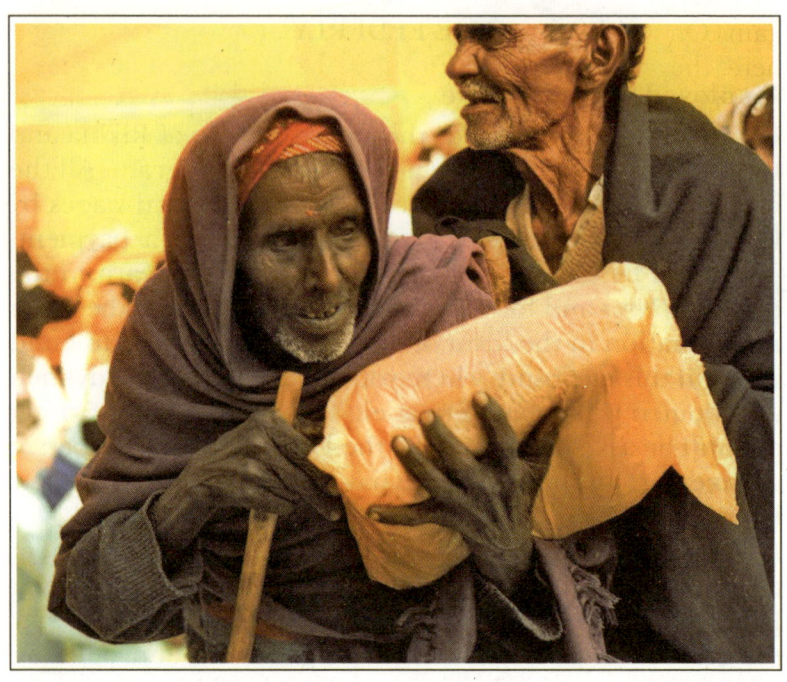

This scheme is very worthwhile. Slowly people will extend their cooperation, and support it. There will be one hundred, then two hundred, then three hundred old people coming in the morning. They will be given malas and will start the japa, *Hare Rama Hare Rama Rama Rama Hare Hare; Hare Krishna Hare Krishna Krishna Krishna Hare Hare*. They will go on for eight hours. In this way they will have a double advantage; they will earn wages and they will also benefit from the japa. I guarantee a rich reward from repeating the name of God. This is a divine idea; it comes from Godly inspiration.

Spiritual ecology
The programs that man implements, like making roads, opening shops, building houses, founding schools and other such things, fetch daily wages of twenty or thirty rupees for the people working on the projects, but there is no spiritual

gain. On the other hand, when old people start doing japa here, they will also receive a spiritual advantage. The biggest benefit will be purification of the atmosphere. Just as a house is constructed with bricks and cement, the atmosphere is created by Rama's name.

The atmosphere has two aspects: physical and spiritual. I am talking about the spiritual ecosystem. The physical ecosystem depends on the spiritual ecosystem. If the spiritual ecosystem of a place gets spoilt then the physical ecosystem cannot improve either. If the people here become too headstrong then nothing will work. However, when there is chanting of the Lord's name by hundreds of thousands of people every day, there will be peace in all four directions.

A sannyasin has a definite influence on people and he must use it for their welfare. There are thousands of panchayats in India. Sannyasins should go to each panchayat, give satsang to the people and organize the recitation of the *Ramayana*. Every *Marga Shirsha*, on *Shukla Panchami*, the fifth day of the bright fortnight, they should also help the villagers to celebrate Sita's marriage and let the people enjoy the name of God being chanted; that's all. If each saint or sannyasin takes moral responsibility for the development of one panchayat in India, there will be no need for a five-year plan any more. We would require only a one-year plan because we would have plenty of resources.

CO-TRAVELLERS SCHEME

Although Bholenath was externally ferocious, internally he was one with me; and believe me, he used to communicate. His eyes used to communicate, his mouth used to communicate his feelings, his emotions, his bhava. In his memory, on full moon days, the old age pension is given to all the elderly of the area.

Swami Niranjan: You know that when Sri Swamiji first came to this area, many people did not have food and clothing. Slowly, Sivananda Math started its activities here with Sri

Swamiji's permission. Now one more scheme has been added. We call it the 'old age pension scheme'.

Sri Swamiji: Not pensioners, co-travellers.

Swami Niranjan: Every month all the co-travellers of Sri Swamiji receive a stipend and clothes, umbrellas or whatever is required, depending upon the season.

Sri Swamiji: We will all require an umbrella. It will be so hot on the way, and it is such a long way from here to the abode of God. Who knows how many years it will take? On the way, we may smoke a few little bidis. If there is money in the pocket then we will eat some nuts as well, because the road is so long. And the biggest thing is that nobody knows the way.

We are travelling to our original home. We are here in this world as visitors for fifty to eighty years, and then ultimately we have to return home. So before we go, I thought, 'Let me have some money and you had better have some money. On the way we will have a little puff and a drink, something like that!' They are all travellers of between seventy and eighty years and some of them have already gone. They got their ticket and we are still on the waiting list.

So, under this scheme, every month the co-travellers are given different things, according to the season. If it is raining, they are given umbrellas. If it is cold, they are given blankets and sweaters.

Swami Niranjan: There are quite a large number of co-travellers as you will see, and each one is given about five hundred and one rupees every month, along with other accessories to facilitate their travel.

Sri Swamiji: This is the scheme that the government of India announced, but I am implementing it. In a very important way, Bholenath is really the founder of the whole scheme. He was a dog, but there was a soul inside him who used to give me proper guidance. Before he left his body, he said, "Swamiji, my work is over. I came here to be a companion in your panchagni sadhana and now that work is complete." In panchagni sadhana the devata Bhairava is there, and the dog is Bhairava. Bhole came here for that period and when his work was over he left. Since that day, the elderly have received their pension every month. And they all receive something extra on the occasion of Sat Chandi Mahayajna.

6

Education

Education is such a thing that it gives the third eye to a nation. If the countries of the West have been able to establish their eminence over the world, it is on the basis of only one thing: education. Education is the foundation of man. Education is the basis of life. Qualification is the basis of life. If a country is qualified, its problems will be solved on their own.

IMPORTANCE OF EDUCATION

Education is the most important thing for a society; no society can rise if its members are not educated. It is what brings prosperity to a house. A human being is born for higher achievements, whether material or spiritual, and education is a tool to bring out an individual's hidden potential. Education is the birthright of every individual, and it is the job of the government to provide its citizens their rights. The way the government provides law through the courts, protection through the army, administration through its machinery, it must provide education to our children. The right to education should be free all over the world. Also, the institutions that provide free education should get tax benefits. Education should not become a business. Flow of money does not make a business. Even our institutions receive money, but we don't run a business.

There is so much poverty in India that people cannot educate their children. Therefore, all of us should contribute a part of our earnings towards education of the less privileged. People should give freely. It is not difficult to spare a part of your earnings. You can stop smoking and divert all your cigarette money towards social upliftment. Contribute in the creation of a school if you can. It is not very difficult to create a small school; the children can go there until the age of fifteen and if a child is brilliant, arrangements can be made for their further education. You can even give toys and games for smaller children. I am not ready to believe that the prosperous cannot spare a part of their wealth for the non-prosperous. You should develop an attitude of sharing. Help the needy and the poor. There are many institutions that you can contribute to.

NEED FOR PRACTICAL EDUCATION

The purpose of education should be twofold. First, it should make the student capable of earning his own bread and butter as early as possible, without spending so many years in school. Second, it should develop the personality so that the student can discover his own self. In the absence of this kind of education there is total anarchy. One of the major reasons for social disorder on every continent is that we have not discovered appropriate forms of education for different types of people.

In India, the schools give nothing more than elementary education. The nation cannot make economic progress unless and until the schools train the students to earn their livelihood. There is no freedom from poverty, families cannot look after their members and elderly parents are neglected because students receive no practical training for their lives.

In the West, I have seen that many children study until eighth grade and then leave school. It is compulsory for them to study until eighth grade and the government enforces these laws. So, even in the West, many children do not go on to higher studies. After eighth or tenth grade they find a job and start to earn money and those who want to study further use this money for their study expenses. Those who are not inclined to study further, do not. In India, since the British Raj, it has become the system to study up to graduation level. People spend ten thousand rupees or more on higher education and then they cannot find a job, nor is their money refunded. This is the fault of our education system and nobody is ready to rectify it.

In the villages, it is sufficient for children to study until eighth or ninth grade or to do their matriculation, tenth grade. I do not believe much in obtaining degrees. If one wants to have a professional career and become an engineer, lecturer, doctor or lawyer, one should go on to advanced studies, but if one wants a simple, contented village life and can manage on a meagre income, it is enough to matriculate.

The first is to equip you with qualifications so you can earn a livelihood in agriculture, commerce or technology. Through education you should receive instruction about the outside world. The second purpose is to impart knowledge about the inner world, by which you can remove the darkness of ignorance within you. This form of education instructs you about yourself, your body and your social dealings. In today's system of education we have neither.

Different types of education

Our present educational system in India needs a lot of change. Education cannot and should not be universal; it has to be modified for different types of people. Here in rural India, it should be oriented towards agriculture because more than seventy percent of the population is based in agriculture. Right from the very beginning, rural children should be taught how to tend a cow or a goat, how bio-gas can be produced, how to cultivate vegetables, grains and fruits, how and when to prepare the soil for crops of various seasons. These things are not taught in the rural schools and the people concerned do not demand this type of practical education from their government. The education system needs to be changed completely so that practical aspects of life are fully covered.

There are primary, middle and high schools here in Rikhia panchayat, but these boys know nothing practical for everyday life. I call the young boys and say, "Go and learn how to drive an autorickshaw, learn how to drive a car." I call the girls and tell them to learn stitching. Sometimes we also teach them stitching and weaving so that they can earn their daily bread. Schools do not teach anything practical and useful. In fact, if the schools were closed, you would lose nothing, rather a lot of money would be saved. School teachers should not be offended, because what I am saying is correct. Gandhi also said the same thing. He emphasized a basic education which is appropriate for different people.

Swami Satsangi is a first-class graduate, but she was not able to tell the difference between a cow and a bull until she came here. I am telling you frankly that whatever I learned at school never proved useful to me either. My father's money was wasted on my education for many years. Had I stopped my academic education and renounced at the age of ten, I could have become another Shankaracharya! I lost those ten young, brilliant years of my life. At the age of eight or ten, one is very bright, and by the age of eighteen or nineteen one is full of conflicts and problems.

I wasted my precious youth learning useless things about geography and history. Whatever I memorized from the history book at night would be completely forgotten by the morning. On the other hand, whatever I learned in the twelve years at my guru's ashram has been useful throughout my life. I took sannyasa at the age of nineteen and lived in my guru's ashram for twelve years and I never used the knowledge that I learned at school. It has proved useless.

The basics of reading, writing and arithmetic, were useful, but beyond that nothing helped me. I never used it. Never!

In Rishikesh, at my guru's ashram, the education was very solid: civil engineering, electrical engineering, accountancy, banking, prayer and worship, driving, and so on. I learned how to carry bundles of firewood, how to use a pickaxe and sickle, how to garden, cook, build a house, keep accounts, do auditing, type and write articles. The most valuable lesson I learned was that life is ever flowing, always moving ahead, that one has to just watch the phenomenal world as it comes and take it in one's stride. I received the kind of training that, no matter what conditions you place me in, I can do the work. Make me the managing director of a company and I will run it, because I know what management is and how it is executed. Even today, when I am by no means young, if I have to open a shop and conduct a business, I can do it. Even the smallest practical teaching proved highly valuable to me until today. What I studied at school was of no use. What did I learn, the names of history's great men. Do you get a job with all this? You get a job through knowhow and action, *artha* and *karma*.

Upgrade the education system
The whole world will have to take a fresh look at education. One type of education will not serve the whole world. In Africa, Latin America, Southeast Asia, China and Central Asia, only one system of education was adopted, which is why there is economic imbalance. There is a lot of intellectual frustration. Students spend many years at college and university, yet they have no jobs when they graduate.

Therefore, those of you living in villages, towns and cities must rethink your education system. You must seriously consider what you need to add or amend in the present education system. If you can see that what is taught in schools today is not at all necessary, then why go on admitting your children and increasing the number of students in schools and colleges? There is a boy sitting here with us who was asked by his teacher the other day where milk comes from. He replied that it came from the dairy. He did not even know that cows yield milk. You will all laugh if I tell you the funny things that are happening around here. All these parents sitting here mutely send their children to missionary schools. All the children learn at school is how to speak in English and Hindi, but they do not know how to milk a cow.

Can a farmer's son, a mason's son, a washerman's son, a carpenter's or a potter's son learn anything about farming, masonry, carpentry or pottery in the village schools? When he finishes middle school has he learned to drive a taxi or autorickshaw? No, he does not pick up these skills at school. If he does learn any skill, it is done privately outside the school. None of the girls from the villages know how to knit or sew. All they learn at school is some irrelevant historical information like what the name of Aurangazeb's daughter was, where Shah Jehan was buried, or when emperor Ashoka invaded Orissa. What does this matter to a poor carpenter, a farmer or a mason? He wants his son to earn as soon as he is eighteen. The son graduates, but he does not know what to do. He does not even know how to drive a car, so he cannot become a taxi driver. In school he is taught about political leaders, kings and queens and how many children they had. This kind of education does not help him at all. These things can be learned later when one is twenty-five or thirty, if there is an interest. Thus, the instruction imparted at school is of no use either in material or in spiritual life, either in the outer or inner world.

I have visited all the educational institutes, missionary schools, gurukuls, Arya Samaj schools, schools run by sadhus and mahatmas. All the schools are competent as far as the three 'R's: reading, writing, arithmetic, are concerned, but they are just not teaching anything of value for life skills. Education must cater to the social and national needs of the time. I am not talking about international matters; I am talking about our own country. India is on the threshold of the twenty-first century, but the mentality of the people is back in the sixteenth century. One comes across many villagers still living the life of the fourteenth century.

Formal study is essential to life, but every child needs to be given knowledge that relates to his life. You study physics and chemistry, but you do not know how to keep your mind under control. You may score ninety-five percent in physics, but if you remain a loser in life what is the use of your study? I am not saying that studying is not important. It is important to make a living, but you must know more about life. When I say 'life', I mean one's body and mind. People do not know who they are; they while away their time in gossip. You should stay away from such useless things.

Requirement of proper facilities

Children are the prospect of the future. They will have to be prepared, not just in the context of one country, but also in the context of the whole world. Whatever you earn, should be used fully to give your children a good, modern and practical education. This means that the principal part of your earnings should be spent on their education. It is essential that children advance in their studies. If a child is not interested in studying, do not take him from school to make him work at something else. Consider what subjects are relevant for his future lifestyle and ensure that he studies those subjects at school. Nowadays, education is of many kinds: sports and modelling are also a kind of education. Sportspeople earn from eight to eighty million rupees a year, whether or not they know the name of their prime minister. Modelling, too, earns a good income, and it also gives a boost to the textile industry.

A boy who has received a BA degree does not even know how to write a job application. Is it possible to get a job only by coming into contact with the 'right' people? It is not as if people are not talented or worthy of jobs. However, the governing system of our country is such that the education system suffers. Many boys in this village want to become something, but cannot, because the facilities do not exist. For any person to become big, for any progress to come about, it is necessary to have the facilities of an education that is in keeping with the times. In our country, education does not keep up with the times. Therefore, education should be such that children are in tune with the present and future society. The future society will be a hi-tech one. The dreams of the current generation are hi-tech too. They may enjoy taking a ride on a bullock cart or elephant for a change, but what they really want is a Mercedes Benz.

Demand and supply

Here in Rikhia, a village woman wears the same sari for six years. There is no demand, because money is necessary for demand. To spend, you have to have the ability to earn. To have the ability to earn, you have to have the skill to earn, and for this the right education is necessary. None of this exists here. In a country where the governing system is good, the education system will also be properly related to the needs of society. If you receive a proper education, you will get a job. If there are jobs, money will be generated. If money is generated, the market will benefit. If the market is benefited, industries will produce more, and the demand and supply chain will go up.

Opportunities and prospects

Children should be taught from an early age how to cope with the demands of day-to-day life according to their particular circumstances. A person in Western Europe has to cope with certain circumstances. In Africa, Asia and Latin America, the circumstances are entirely different. India is an agricultural country. Its education must be oriented towards agriculture, farming, cattle breeding and small business that support the demands of this lifestyle.

It is the job of parents to provide an opportunity for their children. Opportunity means prospects. Prospect comes into effect when the child is able to go forward on his own quest and returns something through the quest. He will then find a place in history; his quest will find a place in history. In today's age, name and fame are not enough; one has to have money too. The two go side by side. Today's age is the age of balance. So, parents should put their children on the path of education, give them the chance to grow and study. This is the extent of your responsibility towards your children. When they grow up, they can look after their own future.

EDUCATION FOR GIRLS

You must remember the feeling of my heart, which I have put into your bags with the reading and writing materials. Try not to forget it. You should always bear in mind that Swamiji wishes you to pursue your studies in the right spirit, earn something, serve society and then enter into family life . . . First is education, second is profession and third is production: marriage and progeny.

In the 1914–1918 War, hundreds of thousands of young men died. There was a second war, from 1939 to 1945, and millions more died. England became devoid of young men, and the girls had to come out and work as bus conductors, to repair telephones, and work in offices. They took their rights themselves. The government cannot give rights to anyone. To gain one's rights one has to deserve them. Girls and boys are equal parts of society and today Indian society has to reconsider whether or not we really appreciate the social value of women and men. As long as women do not stand on an equal platform with men, their country cannot stand upright. To ensure their daughter's rights, every mother and father has the responsibility to see that she is well-educated.

Literacy is not the question. Literacy is not the aim of life; rather, one has to be well-educated. Just as you worry about the education of a boy as soon as he is born, similarly, instead of worrying about a girl's marriage as soon as she is born, worry about her education. The day a girl is educated, she will find her own future. She herself will be able to build her future.

In India, only one member of the family earns to feed the rest of the family and the income is very small, whereas when four people in a family work, they amass four times as much money. In Europe, parents ask their children to fend for themselves after a certain age. They tell their children to stand on their own two feet, so that the parents themselves can have a comfortable and carefree life in their old age. Therefore, Europeans have been able to rule the world, and they have left the stamp of their culture and civilization all over the world. Our own pattern of dress, the wearing of shirts and trousers, our food, the use of telephones and other devices, all reflect the influence of the progressive European culture.

In India, it is just the opposite; the responsibility increases in old age. A householder has to bear the burden of his wife, unmarried daughters and, later on, grandchildren as well. Then there is the added responsibility of a daughter-in-law. Civilization and culture do not progress because of the male population alone. Civilization progresses when both men and women contribute to it equally, and when there is one hundred percent literacy.

The amount budgeted for the education of a girl should be the same as the amount budgeted for the education of a boy. Through education, girls should fulfil their dreams of becoming something. A girl is more responsible than a boy is; this is the view of the psychologists. Scientists have said that the brain centres for *viveka buddhi*, discrimination between right and wrong, are well developed in women. A person who has this *viveka shakti*, or discriminative force, only needs to be well-educated.

Educate the village girls
When I tell the village girls to learn to read and stand on their own two feet, they reply that it is of no use to them, as they will only be cooking, cleaning, washing and begetting children anyway when they get married. Education does not help them in these chores at all. The majority of them are not interested in going to school for the sake of learning. They are attracted only by the free midday meal provided by the government. They are not serious about book learning. This is the reply twelve-year-old girls give me. Therefore, day and night we say, "Educate the girls more than the boys." We are pressing this point in order to give more importance, more rights and more freedom to girls than to boys.

In the past, we were doing it all wrong. I am saying this not because I am a social reformer, but because we are poor people. Labourers working in big cities can easily earn more than fifteen hundred rupees a year, but local labourers can hardly earn four hundred. A labourer who works here cannot even afford to go forty kilometres to Bhagalpur to visit his guru. How much poverty prevails here! The cause of poverty is the deficiency of Lakshmi, and women are Lakshmi, not men. In the first mantra of *Saundarya Lahari* it is written: *Shivah shaktya yukto yadi bhavati shaktah prabhavitum* – "Without Shakti, even Shiva is ineffective."

The manifest form of Shakti is the female, the girl, the sister, the daughter, the wife, the mother, and we males have made her a cripple. We have cut her wings, because during the Middle Ages another influence was thrust upon us. We had to adjust ourselves to that political influence then, but now the times have changed.

Nowadays, we are living in a modern civilization where our girls have many options. Earlier, in every society, whether eastern or western, there was only one future for girls: to grow up, get married and produce children. The options of studying or setting up a business did not exist. Today all these opportunities are open. They can study, acquire knowledge and obtain a degree: BA, MA, LLB, BCom, MCom, BSc, MSc, become doctors, engineers, learn about computers and electronics and be well versed in biotechnology. They can become businesswomen, industrialists or social workers, stand up in the Supreme Court and argue a case, or run for election and sit in Parliament. A woman can become president, chief of the army staff, a scientist, a space traveller or revolutionary. She can pick up a gun. Our daughters can do anything. In today's society, girls can talk freely with boys. Nobody infers that there must be something cooking between them; that society has gone, and such a society should go, otherwise your society cannot advance.

The tradition of differentiating between education of boys and girls should end, and if the affluent take the lead in this cause, it will be better. The poor cannot do this work. There is a saying, "Who will bell the cat?" Only a cat can bell a cat, not a mouse. So start this process.

Mother is the first guru

Until the age of seven years, the mother is the guru of the child. She is responsible for the development of all the desired qualities, such as love, compassion and intelligence. Just as the gardener looks after a small plant, she too

provides for the total care and nutrition of the child. The compost and manure are derived from her blood and bone marrow. She is like the farmer who gives urea to the plant when it is growing. Once the plant is fully grown, urea is no longer useful. In the same way, giving nutrition to a baby is the mother's responsibility, and that nutrition does not mean only feeding, it is all-inclusive. How to manage and take care of the child's eyes, for example. If the eyes develop a squint after birth then the mother can correct it, because the body is amenable to change at that time. The education which a child receives up to the age of seven years is maternal, internal or emotional education.

Traditionally, when the training which the mother is supposed to impart finishes, the child is then sent to the guru or acharya. The rite which is conducted at that time is known as *upanayan samskara*. The word 'upanayan' comes from the root *nayan*, which means 'the physical eye which perceives other forms, objects, colours and everything in the external nature, be it sky or earth'. However, this physical eye does not help to see the thoughts inside. *Upa* plus 'nayan' means the 'second eye which is needed to see the thoughts'. Initiation into that training is upanayan samskara and initially both sexes were given this samskara.

In the age when girls also went to the gurukul to study, they also wore the thread and did Gayatri japa. Now the times have changed. The men could see that if women sat for japa, no one would make the bed, clean and wash, bring the tea, cook, or milk the cows. Therefore, they decided that she had to become their maid and thought, "Better we wear her thread as well." So, the male became the bearer of six threads instead of three.

Gender bias

Today, in rural India, most women do not work to earn money. They do household work worth about four or five hundred rupees per month, but if a girl is educated and works outside, she can easily earn four to five thousand rupees. Then she can afford four hundred rupees for a maid. Indian women do not work and, therefore, they do not have money and cannot have any independence. In Europe, every adult man or woman works and earns his or her livelihood and has an opportunity to live independently and separately.

Indians have been set back due to gender bias. They have a different set of rules for boys and girls. Purely because of their gender, girls are not allowed to do many things and as a result they remain ignorant and do not become worldly-wise. In Europe, there is more technology and wealth because of education and freedom for women. They do not keep boys and girls apart. When the male and female children both grow in the same womb, when both come into the world from the same pathway, why should they be separated? God has not done this, so why should we?

When the girls saw Swami Satsangi speaking English so fluently, they were surprised. They were even more astonished when they saw her driving vehicles. Thus, they followed suit and the process of education among the girls began. The girls of this area now go to Deoghar, eight kilometres away, on bicycles, which have been provided by this ashram. In my opinion, education in this age is tantamount to having the third eye, *jnana chakshu*. No society can prosper without that education. Without education, a society cannot march forward.

People say girls should be educated, but no one considers the difficulties they face in their studies. Therefore, many girls abandon their studies and do not graduate. If a girl from here goes to college ten or fifteen kilometres away from home and has no means of transportation, we give her a bicycle, so that she can study. She belongs to a backward class and so it will be good if she graduates. A few more good people will be added to our society, otherwise hooliganism will continue to increase.

Education and profession before marriage

Wherever I go I favour women. All the girls like me, because I say, "Go and get educated, go to university, go to college, graduate." Society discourages them. These girls should be properly educated and trained. You must all study hard. Then they can find a job and stand on their own two feet. They can hold a job in a bank, in schools and colleges, become doctors or lawyers, a collector or a superintendent of police. After they have done that, or even along with establishing a career, those who wish to marry and set up house should do so. There is no harm in marrying. This is a matter to understand. I never prohibit marriage, but I must reiterate that marriage is not the only future for a girl. A hundred years ago marriage might have been a proposition, but now their future lies in higher education and they can have a future on many fronts.

If the social aspirations of children are not left up to them but dictated by us, we will carry their burden as well. We will feel burdened and the children will feel suffocated their whole life through. This is what happened in the past with our mothers and wives. From the psychological point of view, they were a complex-ridden sex. Society must give its children the chance to express their talent if the country is to progress.

The problem is that these children have ambitions, but their parents are ill-bred and ill-informed. They cannot see beyond their noses. The village girls of this area tend domestic cattle, collect the cow dung in the early morning, graze the cattle and goats and by the time they are eighteen or nineteen they are the mothers of two or three children. To beget a number of children was the necessity of the past,

when our society was primitive and agriculture was the mainstay. Now the times have changed and children have ambitions. They talk among themselves of their dreams and ambitions; however, their parents cannot see beyond begetting children. They don't know how to plan their families or how to make sacrifices for the wellbeing of their offspring.

There are many fathers who drink beyond their means and leave nothing for their wives and children. They say, "What will the children do after they have received higher education?" I asked one of the fathers to send his daughter to school. Quick came the reply, "What will she do after getting an education? Will she do anything other than dealing with the cow dung?" This idea of education is very prevalent in society; it is not an insignificant idea.

Treasure of learning

The children here are learning to read and write in the schools. I want you all to go on pursuing your studies sincerely and become self-reliant. Today you will all receive prasad. There are notebooks in your schoolbag, a geometry set, pens and pencils. Your bag also contains a T-shirt and trousers, and one invisible thing: my feelings and my blessings. You may not see that, but the feeling of my heart is there.

In the twentieth sloka of *Neetishatak*, Bhartrihari states:

Vidyanaam narasye roopamadhikam prachchhahnaguptam dhanam
Vidya bhogkari yashah sukhakari vidya gurunam guruh
Vidya bandhujano videshgamane vidya paramdaivatam

Learning is man's abundant beauty, it is his hidden treasure. Learning is a source of enjoyment, fame and pleasure, learning is the super preceptor. While in a foreign country learning is your friend and guide. Learning is supreme fortune.

I have travelled in foreign countries. Swami Vivekananda travelled in foreign countries. We won the world by dint of our learning and knowledge. Learning, knowledge and wisdom are required to win the world. Therefore, you should take a keen interest in your studies and acquire knowledge to stand on your own feet. You should motivate your parents also to learn something. Devote more time to your studies.

Opportunity for success

I have to give the same message to the boys also. Avoid idle rambling; avoid the company of cigarette smokers, tobacco chewers and those youngsters who are fond of liquor. Maintain a respectful distance from those idlers who have no stake in life. If you have to fashion a decent future, you should take your career seriously. I am particularly addressing the young boys. The government has offered a number of concessions to the backward classes. You must try to avail yourselves of these concessions without resorting to underhand methods.

I give books and stationery to a number of boys and girls admitted to St Francis and Ramakrishna Mission Schools. I am working on many projects to promote education in this area. You must remember the feeling of my heart, which I have put into your bags with the reading and writing materials. Try not to forget it. You should always bear in mind that Swamiji wishes you to pursue your studies in the right spirit, earn something, serve society and then enter into family life. Entering into holy wedlock and producing children should be relegated to the last option. Marriage and children should never be your first priority. Try to remember that marriage and progeny should be your last priority. First is education, second is profession and third is production: marriage and progeny.

MEANINGFUL CHANGE

One day, a little girl from the nearby village of Nawadih said, "Swamiji, I want to learn English." I said to Swami Satsangi, "Look here, this is your breakthrough: English." Swami Satsangi started with one girl and now you can see for yourself how the number has grown to almost two thousand. There is a big demand and their parents press her daily to enrol their children to learn English. When she asked them what they wanted to learn, they did not opt for Hindi or Sanskrit, their unanimous choice was English.

Now the local girls attend classes here in the ashram for six months a year. The multiplication tables are all spoken in English. They do not say, "Do ekam do, do dooni chaar, do tiya chhah," they say, "two ones are two, two twos are four, two threes are six," and so on. All the students read in English. They not only read English, but practise it too. Whenever I come across them during my morning stroll, they say, "Good morning, Swamiji," and also enquire, "How are you?" When I ask how they are, they say, "Fine." We should not decide what the language of our country should be. It should be decided by the labourers, because a labourer is pragmatic, he is practical. He is close to reality.

Therefore, these children now speak English. They also sing English songs and we have arranged music and singing classes. There is a big classroom for them here and they now sing that English song, "Come here, my dear, Krishna Kanhai." The day is not far off when they will sing pop songs too, and this pop music has a very good rhythm. Our mother tongue is Sanskrit, not Hindi. Now, if you cannot speak Sanskrit, which is a beautiful language, you can get a lot of pleasure from speaking in English. People even dream in English these days! English is the most widely spoken language in the world. Today, if you want to read a book on any subject, it will be available in English, whether it is religious or spiritual, the Vedas or *Ramayana*. Many of the scriptural texts have been translated into English by great scholars like Swami Vivekananda, Sri Aurobindo, Swami Sivananda and Bhagavat Prabhupad, and they are very authentic.

We have also introduced computer lessons and inducted a few kanyas who are good in English for computer training. They have learnt to operate computers so fast that some of them are now ready to teach the smaller children. I have been promised any number of computer monitors by well-wishers. Then, what do I need? If I get one hundred or two hundred monitors and hard drives, hundreds of students in this panchayat will be computer literate. As far as teachers are concerned, there is no problem, because everyone here knows computers, all these gerudharis know computers. This is the influence of spiritual life on them, this is the sign that their kundalini is awakening!

Study has become their passion, and the proof is that a private school has opened in our panchayat where parents pay a daily fee of thirty rupees to have their children educated. This shows how keen they are to have their children educated. The local administration does not have to tell them to do that, as they now understand the value of education. In the earlier years when I offered the village women the *Ramayana* they told me they could not read. Nevertheless, when I told them to learn to read it they did so in two or three months. Now, all those village women sitting there can read that book very well, though they persist in saying that they cannot. And their children have developed an intense interest in their studies and their education.

When I first arrived in Rikhia, neither the children nor their parents showed any interest in studies. I was surprised because my feeling was that if the sannyasins in the ashram are so highly educated, then householders and their children should also be knowledgeable. We have arranged classes for teaching English, which start from Makar Sankranti, 14th January each year. People from Patna, Bangalore and other places come and spend their time here teaching these very small children from the surrounding villages. Almost all the children come from labourers' families, where the breadwinner pulls a rickshaw or a thela, or is a coolie, or a ploughman or weaves mats.

When we came here, all the schools were empty with practically no attendance, but today they are so keen to learn and study that there is full attendance in the nearby schools! Now the schools are overflowing with children, and the local administration has also made a few nice classrooms for them. We give them all the books they require and we have put up educational charts for them.

Today is the third day of the yajna and prasad will be distributed to approximately nine hundred children from the middle schools. Their parents and other family members have already received their prasad. The whole area will be teeming with children and we will offer the children what they deserve for their education. Oh, what a sight it will be! Every year we give them school bags, reading, writing and painting materials, notebooks, coloured pencils, pastels, erasers, pencil sharpeners, instrument boxes, games and toys, everything they will need for one year of study, including school uniforms. Once the local education officer was passing by one of his own government schools and he was surprised to find all the boys and girls in uniform. When he enquired from the teachers whether it was a new Christian missionary school, he was flabbergasted to learn that it was one of his own government schools. He was very happy because no government school provides uniforms for the children. He came and thanked me.

7

Health

When our clinic was being established, there was a proposal to provide a village health centre with all the modern medical facilities. I said, "No, better to have a clinic that provides only the basic facilities. If you have to take an X-ray, or if blood and stool or urine need to be examined, or if some major surgery is essential, send the patient to Deoghar or wherever necessary." In this way, we can run our clinic by catering to a wide variety of patients without administrative overheads and other problems. We simply pay the money for the medical services rendered from other medical experts. In this way, we can engage the help of the local medical doctors and amenities. Suppose a villager requires an X-ray. We send them to an established X-ray clinic in Deoghar, the X-ray is taken, the report is given and we then determine the necessary treatment. We simply pay for the X-ray bill.

After all, an X-ray costs about one hundred rupees, but if you have to keep an X-ray machine, you also need a complete maintenance system. You will require very good staff and then you have to arrange for their stay, their payment and all kinds of things, according to the rules of the government and income tax return and direct taxes. All kinds of support services are required and then the establishment becomes too big. I do not want that because big establishments are not able to help the people.

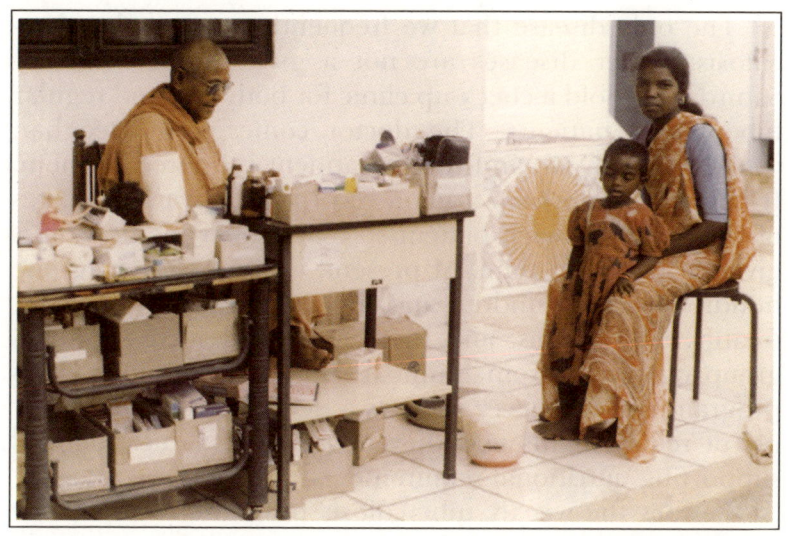

So, our clinic here is of a new type. In Deoghar, we have many doctors, pathologists, X-ray clinics and surgeons. Whenever we find someone needs them, we just phone to make an appointment and send them there. They treat the person and send the bill to us and that works efficiently, and it is cheaper too. Even in India, medical treatment and medicines have become very costly, and my neighbours would not be able to afford medical treatment if they had to pay for it. At our clinic the village people do not have to pay for treatment, so we always have patients.

Local ailments

There may be many poor people here who cannot afford medicine, but what about the countries which have the best medical care? Their citizens are sicker than these poor people here. In rural India, the medical problems are not as serious as you have in big cities or in places like England, Europe, the US, Germany and other western countries: AIDS, heart problems, nervous diseases. Villagers generally do not have diabetes or heart disease, and blood pressure is practically zero because the lifestyle in the rural set up is different.

The only disease that we frequently confront is tuberculosis. Other diseases are not a great problem. Every Saturday we hold a check-up clinic for both new and regular tuberculosis patients. The doctor comes from Deoghar, examines them all, and then treatment is offered to them. It is necessary to keep a good record of the various stages of treatment for each patient so that proper medication is given at the right time. At present, we are registering one hundred to one hundred and fifty patients in our regular treatment programs, and there is a good success rate. A group of people from Mumbai sponsors this tuberculosis program and whenever there is a need, we send them our list of requirements and they deliver the medication and supporting nutritional requirements.

Besides the weekly tuberculosis program, we open the clinic on Sundays specifically to treat children; women, including pregnant women, are seen on Fridays, and the general health needs of the panchayat are catered to on the other days of the week. We mostly treat waterborne diseases, skin infections, nutritional deficiencies and stomach disorders. There are also seasonal sicknesses like fever, cough and cold. That is all. These are the major health problems here. Of course, there are burns, and often serious burns related to cooking on open fires. Scorpion and snakebites are also common. Villagers have rural ailments which do not involve expensive treatments. A few medicines, quinine and injections are good enough to cure them; and they do not consume large quantities of Vitamin A, B, C and D, as is common in the western lifestyle.

Health camps

From time to time, once or twice a year, we have what you call 'camps': eye camps, dental camps – they are very popular. We operate them here for one day, two days or three days and then send the patients home. Each camp draws about one to two hundred patients from around the district. If an old man goes blind, what can be done? If it is a small child, we can send him to Kolkata, Munger or elsewhere for specialist consultation and treatment. In most cases, however, these people do not need outside treatment, and if it is offered to them, they refuse it.

Hard constitutions

We have a very good dispensary here, for which medicines come from Australia, New Zealand, Mumbai, Delhi and other places, but we have to give away many of these medicines in Deoghar, because they do not get used. The people here just do not fall sick. We give away all the medicines for diabetes; it does not exist here. In western countries, the alternate therapies like homeopathy, acupuncture, reiki, and others are very popular, but here they are not accepted. They only want modern medicines, what you call allopathic; not even ayurveda is popular. They do not believe in alternate therapies and if you give them anything other than allopathic medicine, it does not work on them because they are not soft people.

The village people have a very hard constitution; they work physically the whole day. Many walk from this place to Deoghar every day, ten, fifteen and twenty kilometres with a load, and then return the same day. They eat whatever they get and their staple diet generally consists of salt and rice. Nevertheless, they have the strength to work the whole day at physical labour. They rise at four am and walk to faraway fields to evacuate their bowels. They bathe in the pond and sweep their own homes. They carry bricks, plough fields and work the whole day through. I am a witness to their state of health. The food that you eat is believed to contain all the necessary nutrients, yet you fall sick. So it is not necessary that strength-producing food is also health-producing. More important than the kind of food eaten is the assimilation of food in the body. This means that every part, every nutrient of the food must reach the right place. This is the merit of hard labour. In the villages, they are physically active from before dawn until after sunset and do not need a sleeping pill to fall asleep. When one does physical work, every part of the body from the head to the toes is managed, the way a machine is completely repaired. Every part is cleaned; all the nadis, granthis and muscles of the body are cleansed through physical action.

Life here is natural, so they do not need any pranayama or asana. Only when life becomes unnatural do you need naturopathy to correct it. You need to practise asana and pranayama, and watch what you eat because you are carrying damaged material. Therefore, I have made only one rule for those who live here: work the whole day long, work so hard that you fall asleep the moment you hit the bed. Such tiredness is bliss; it is *ananda*.

Alternate therapies like homeopathy, reiki and yoga only work for very delicate people, for soft people, not for hard people. The villagers love injections. When a swami from Germany was staying here, he developed a fever and when he was asked to take an injection, he refused, but if the servants and labourers have fever and you give them an injection, they will recover in no time. That is the difference here. As you say in the West, all modern drugs have side effects, but the local people do not believe that. Those that are educated always say that everything, good or bad, has side effects. Suppose you drink water. It quenches your thirst but its side effect is that you have to urinate more. They say everything has a side effect and that is the law of nature: then why only allopathic medicine? Therefore, they are not worried about side effects. Many people who practise homeopathy offer their services here, but they do not survive more than a day because nobody comes to them again. The villagers say, "We do not want sugar pills."

I can tell you one thing. There is the hard constitution, the soft constitution and the weak constitution, and the local people definitely belong to the hard constitution. The hard sicknesses which they suffer are not presented to a medically trained doctor. Those sicknesses are treated by magic and sorcery. You might call it spiritual healing or psychic healing. For example, hysteria; they will never bring it to a medical doctor. No! Nor snake bites, they will not bring this to a medical doctor. They only trust them with fever and cold, diarrhoea and dysentery and stomach-ache, belching, vomiting and this kind of thing. This attitude not only holds here in Rikhia or India, but throughout the world. The whole of Africa, from Egypt down to Capetown; South America, from Colombia down to Argentina; and the entire Southeast Asia, South Asia, Central Asia, have the same attitude to these sicknesses.

I think that humankind cannot look after all the problems of people in the developing nations. No government can look after all their problems; no institution can look after all their problems of sickness and poverty, lack of education and many, many more things. The whole of Africa is in turmoil. Go from Colombia down to Argentina and through all countries where they may have been able to manage minimal health care, and you will find that mental diseases are growing very quickly. Even if their governments can control physical diseases through good medical establishments, what can they do about the mental cases? Whether a man is rich or poor, from a modern country or developing country, he has some problems.

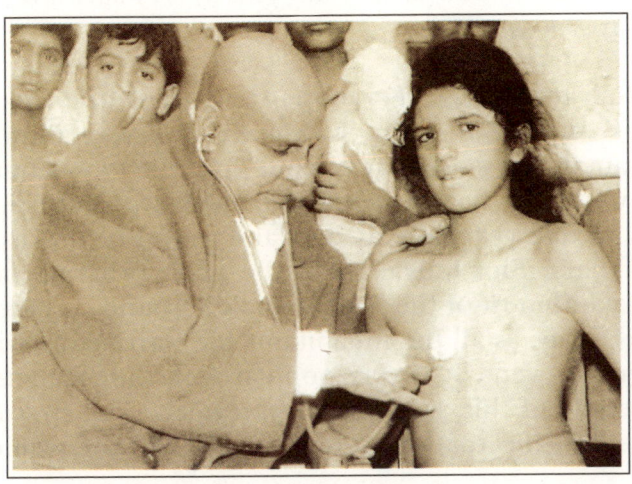

8
Marriage

SITA KALYANAM

The purpose of organizing this grand wedding ceremony is significant and meaningful. In this region, a girl child in the family is considered to be a matter of anxiety and worry. For poor parents, daughters are a burden because it is beyond their means to get them married. The rich do not have this problem, but marriage is an extremely costly affair for the poor and needy. Therefore, I decided to ease their burden by organizing Sita's wedding, thereby doing good to the young brides of these families. Through this wedding celebration I ensure the welfare of many young girls whom I have accepted as my own daughters.

Sita Kalyanam is a very important event and tradition of this Alakh Bara. Sita Kalyanam is a very important program in the sense that it is our program to welcome the newlyweds who have entered this panchayat since the last wedding one year ago, as part and parcel of this ashram and akhara. Sita Kalyanam is the main program of this akhara and most of the houses in and around this area are locked today, as all the inhabitants have arrived to witness this grand event. It is very popular with the villagers and the people of this area like it very much. The crowd that you see on the road is witness to this. All the women in

this area are excited. In every house they are talking about this marriage. Not only in my area, but also in all the surrounding villages, they are talking about Sita's wedding. They are saying that Swamiji is conducting the marriage, and yesterday I put on my wedding costume. This is the talk of every home because they have never seen me wearing a wrapper; they have only seen me in a loincloth.

Dwiragaman, second arrival

In India, usually the marriage takes place when the girl is fifteen or sixteen years old at the most, but the ultimate departure for her husband's home takes place at the age of eighteen or nineteen. It is a special ceremony called *dwiragaman,* second arrival. The first arrival at the husband's home is when she is married and then she returns and stays in her parents' home. The second arrival is when she goes to her husband's home to stay for good.

All the girls who go to their husband's homes after marriage come and see me at Sita Kalyanam, and this has become a complicated routine. On this auspicious day of the marriage of Sita with Lord Rama, *Vivaha Panchami*, the Akhara honours the dwiragaman of all the daughters-in-law of this panchayat with a gift. This is not an ordinary gift; marriage is a samskara, just like birth and *namakaran*, the naming ceremony. I keep very nice things for them, including a gold ornament, which is a must. We call this gift a 'bridal kit', a 'good luck kit'. It contains dresses, jewellery, silver, pearls, clothes, shoes, ornaments, perfumes, lipstick, hair oil, mirror, comb, soap, vermilion and all the other items comprising the *solah shringara*, the sixteen items of beautification. It is a matter of joy for me to give this gift and it is a joy for their parents also, because each kit will cost about fifty thousand rupees. Sometimes it costs more if you include pure gold.

In all, there are sixteen and I add one more item, sanitary towels, which is the seventeenth. Perhaps the ancient rishis and munis did not think of that. The villagers understand this very well. Sometimes they say, "Swamiji, are you giving sixteen items?" I say, "No, seventeen," but they still ask for sixteen although they know the seventeenth. I collect sanitary towels and tampons. Bundles and bundles are kept in the store because it is as important as lipstick, or maybe more so. I have also sent nappies in advance for the expected babies. This idea was someone else's idea, not mine, but the newly-married couples accept this as a propitious omen with Swamiji's blessings to have healthy and gifted babies. If Swamiji has presented a nappy in advance, the baby must come with high hopes.

We have been offering these things for many years. The number of daughters-in-law varies from year to year; sometimes it is two hundred, sometimes three hundred. One year it swelled to six hundred, but still I did not run out of money! This year, however, there will be about one hundred; for some reason fewer marriages have taken place.

Purpose of Sita Kalyanam

I organized Sita's marriage in order to inspire all the visiting parents to give at least a few sets of beautiful items. This is the reason why Sita's wedding was organized. The idea came to this creative mind and the work is now close to completion.

When I first thought of Sita Kalyanam, nobody understood the purpose behind it. In the month of January a bright idea came: 'Sita's marriage'. If I conduct Sita's marriage on the 4th of December, I will definitely get lots of things because a girl's marriage is the obsession of every Indian family.

In the first year of Sita Kalyanam, I asked the mukhia, the chief of the village, to provide a list of all the newly-married girls who are on their way to their husbands' homes. He gave me the names of two hundred and fifty such brides. I told him to spread the news that all these brides would be gifted with good luck kits on the occasion of Sita Kalyanam. To give such precious gifts to so many girls is not a joke. One piece of jewellery that is compulsory for all married women in India is the mangalasutra. All these women are wearing it. *Sutra* means thread and *mangala* means auspicious. All married women in India must have that auspicious thread. It is the symbol of a married woman in India. The mangalasutra is made of gold and some are inlaid with diamonds, pearls and many precious stones. To give such gifts to five or ten girls is one thing, but when the number of girls went up to several hundred, I had to think about how to manage it.

At that time I had nothing to offer them. My coffers were empty, yet I went ahead and extended the invitation to all the young girls in the vicinity. Each of these brides is 'Sita', and Sita will go to her in-law's house. All the houses in and around this Akhara are her husband's houses. All the gifts that you bring have been blessed by Devi at the yajna and will now go to Sita and will reach her husband's houses.

Every girl is my daughter

Once we announced it as the occasion of Sita's wedding, we were flooded with gift items. I received many things. Bundles and bundles of gifts started pouring in. In fact, we had no place to store them. Several centres fulfilled the target by sending 108 good luck kits each. Whenever Swami Niranjan or Swami Satsangi come to me, the first questions I ask are, "Have you put the labels on the suitcases? Have you checked the jewellery? Is it real or artificial?" I had it checked by experts, "Is the sari of good quality? Have you opened it? Is there any defect in it?"

I open and inspect each and every set, and I tell them to add this or change that. In one set there was no cloth for the blouse or petticoat. We have been busy making sets that include mangalasutra, *nathani*, nose-ring, *kangan*, bracelet, and *bichiya*, toe ring. All the village women put on toe rings because they work in the fields. During the paddy season, the women stand in water and mud for long hours and the toes have to be separated, otherwise they become rotten. I am as concerned about the whole affair as if all these girls were my own daughters. I must think that each girl is my daughter or my sister but, of course, not my mother.

This is the emotion of a father, not of a son. It is the father who looks after the marriage of the daughter; it is the brother who looks after the marriage of the sister. This is the emotion of a father or a brother and in this way you are actually training your emotions in the right direction. Only when you train your emotions in the right direction can they be transformed and converted into bhakti, otherwise most of you are totally dissipated. You do not know which way to drive the car. You have a chariot with four horses, one horse goes to the right, another to the left, the third one pulls up and the fourth will not move. Now which way will your chariot go? The untrained senses, mind and emotions all have to be channelled properly.

So, from this, you should now understand that whatever work you undertake must have a good intention, a purpose of doing good to others. I have been harping on this single point, and now that we have started our work here, others will also see and appreciate how good work for humanity is possible through yajnas and how good people from faraway places meet each other at yajnas.

The point is this: I am only passing on to them the gifts that you have given. It is not mine. It is you who have given it as bhet. *Bhet* is the art of giving and receiving. So they will be receiving, as prasad, the bhet that you have offered. Bhet has been converted into prasad like the monsoon is transformed into rain. You gifted, you offered, and it has been given as prasad on behalf of the Devi, after the pooja. At the culmination of this yajna these daughters-in-law, my daughters-in-law, your daughters-in-law and every wise man's daughters-in-law will be felicitated. May God bless them. May they receive more suitcases, may they receive more money, may they receive more bounty and more prosperity.

PROPER MARRIAGE OF GIRLS

The Indian marriage tradition continues with the poorest of the poor people. They will not deviate from their tradition, even if they have to borrow money or sell their jewellery. The marriage ceremony is to be completed in the full traditional way, and any festivity is to be done as per the established custom. If this culture disappears because of poverty, then it is meaningless whether Indians remain united or otherwise.

The Hindu system of marriage is very scientific, although it seems very orthodox, puritanical and strange. Scientifically it is the best system, because when you talk about genetic integration you should always think about the generations ahead, not only about your own child. You have to think of the many future generations and whether this genetic integration will survive for seven generations or not.

There are two types of cultures: robust and fragile. A fragile culture should be handled with care. With a robust culture it does not matter. You can turn it upside down or sideways, roll it or throw it and it will not break. We want that robust culture. No matter if it is rich or poor, literate or illiterate, we do not care. Let the country remain illiterate, but the culture has to be robust, because political history and the ravages of time will not pardon anyone. History meets with accidents. Egypt met with an accident, Greece and Rome met with accidents. Historical accidents are not infrequent and it is very important that the robust cultures of humankind be preserved. The mantra for preserving the seed of this culture is, "Have your daughter married at the right time, to a proper person, in a very proper way." This is the dharma of our culture, religion, society and nation, and the dharma of all parents.

First obligation to society
In all civilizations and cultures throughout the world, those that have gone and those that have stayed, emphasis has

always been laid on the marriage of women. To help with a daughter's marriage is your first dharma. In our country, to marry a daughter is the most important of all duties. That is the top ranking duty. If you cannot marry your daughter properly, you are not paying your proper obligation to society. You have to give your daughter's hand in marriage. The culture of India teaches us, this is your duty and obligation too.

A girl should be married properly because she is the creator of quality. She can create a Rasputin or a Hitler and she can create a Christ or a Rama. It is she who created Buddha and she who created demons. She can create something of quality or something substandard. Therefore, care must be taken regarding her marriage. From the moment a girl is born, especially in India, her parents are obsessed with the idea of her marriage. For ten, twenty or thirty years, until she is married, they keep thinking about it. It was the same in Europe during earlier times. In Asia, a

girl's marriage is still an obsession for the parents, because throughout the history and development of their culture, they have realized that the girl is the most important member of human society. She is the most precious jewel; therefore, it is the duty of every parent to see that she is given to a man in a proper way.

In vedic culture there was no divorce. It was accepted that problems arose in the family between the husband and wife, but the Vedas did not allow divorce. They said that if a husband and wife could not get along together, they may live separate lives, but the question of remarriage did not arise. Of course, I know life is not smooth sailing. There are always quarrels in the family due to differences between husband and wife, which is natural.

As you die once, so you marry once. This is what we think. When I meet the young widows from time to time, I ask them, "Why don't you remarry? You have a problem because there is nobody to maintain you. So you work like a labourer and you have to work very hard." They reply, "It doesn't matter, Swamiji. We can live in poverty. We can eat only once a day. We can wear shabby clothes, but we don't feel like remarrying." I have come across many women like that. This is a problem in India, not because society does not allow widows to remarry, but because they themselves prefer not to. I am not talking about educated girls, they have a different mentality.

The bond between husband and wife does not break, even in the grave, not even after death. This is the ideal form of marriage and must be adhered to. The reason for this was very simple. A woman wants stability, security, and power. Not only in India, but everywhere in the world, a woman wants stability. She wants to stay in one place and not move from there. A woman wants security wherever she comes from, whether Africa, Asia, Europe or any other part of the world. The third thing she wants is to rule. She wants to be the *gharwali*, not the owner but the ruler.

Inheritance rights

In our country, ownership is not a problem because when a girl is married, she takes her inheritance with her in the form of gold, silver, diamonds and pearls. In the West this is called a 'dowry'. We do not call it a dowry, we call it her inheritance. The word is *dahej*, meaning *daibhag*. *Dai* means that it is to be given to her, that it is her right, and *bhag* means part. My daughter, your daughter, everybody's daughter has the right of inheritance to her parents' property. However, you cannot give her one acre of land, as it is immovable; hence you give her gold, silver, pearls, diamonds and cows. Nowadays, a car, television set, radio, washing machine and other things in vogue are given. So, a girl should not be sent out of the family with an empty suitcase. That is not the tradition in India.

In India, even the poorest family that has difficulty obtaining daily meals spends with an open heart and open hands at the time of marriage. Everyone becomes generous. At the marriage time of your daughter, sister or any female member of the family, you must sign a blank cheque because it is her right. Thus, ownership does not come into the picture; she is already the owner. According to recent law, a girl has rights to the property of her parents, not just to the jewels. If you have to sell a part of your land today, you cannot transfer or sell it without the signature of your daughter, because she is a partner in your property, even after her marriage.

Even a girl from a poor family should leave her parents' home with a full suitcase, with a wedding dowry given in the form of jewellery, ornaments, beautiful saris and other necessary articles. This is not a marriage tax. Many people joke about it, saying it is necessary to pay a marriage tax, but the dowry is not given in that spirit. You spend so much money on your son and he becomes a vagabond. He does so many reprehensible things. What have you given to your daughter? We must look after this community of women, so that they will become good mothers, and our future generations will be of a better quality.

THE SCIENCE OF MATCHMAKING

The concept of genetic transfer is at the root of Indian culture. Previously, all marital contracts were decided on this basis alone. Nowadays, marriages do not necessarily take place in this way; many happen on the basis of love. However, love is not a biological factor, it is an emotional factor. It is not emotion or thought, but the biological substance, the sperm and the ovum which produces a child. If I am in love with someone, that is perfectly all right, but the progeny which we produce will be determined by the sperm and ovum, which is the basis of genetic transfer.

Therefore, finding a partner for marriage is a science. The coming together of a man and woman in sexual interaction has to be scientifically investigated, but nobody has the time, and love is blind. I have studied the system of marriage in vedic dharma, the theories of gotra, pravara and guna. According to the astrological system, there are thirty-

six qualities in a person and they have to match to some extent in both partners for positive genetic transfer. This is the astrological and also the psychological theory behind the traditional form of marriage.

Genetic factors

The system of marriage is very important and one should not underrate it, because the quality of progeny depends on it. Every sinner, saint, rogue, dacoit, blind or handicapped person, whether high or low, is born of a mother. That birth is the result of the interaction between a man and a woman, and the fertilization of a small seed. When that seed is born, what type of mental program will accompany it? What type of heart and what type of organs is it bringing? This body is a complex technology and, therefore, this genetic transfer needs to be studied from a scientific basis.

You must marry a person who is *agotra*, who does not belong to your community of genes. There are rules and regulations, family shastras, regarding dharma. People in India, in Gujarat, Orissa, Bengal, Bihar and South India still follow this tradition, although it is gradually withering away. Perhaps they do not all produce the perfect progeny, but at least they do not produce criminals like Rasputin. India has instead produced people like Gandhi, Ishwarchand Vidyasagar, Lokamanya Tilak, Ranade, Raja Rama Mohan Roy, Ramakrishna, Vivekananda and Aurobindo. We need to know more about this subject, and now there are many good books available on it. In particular, there is a magazine published by Gurukul Kangri, Haridwar, a university which is about one hundred years old.

Marriage matching is a very difficult science in terms of genetic transfer. The prime purpose of marriage is not for two people to meet and fall in love with each other. That is the means, not the end. The end product is progeny. You may love somebody, but do not base your marriage on that emotion alone. Love is your private affair; however, from the scenario of marriage, this affair of love does not work. Just because you love a person does not mean that you should marry him or her. Compatibility of the genetic factor, in addition to the cultural factor, should be considered.

Marrying outside your community or country is not a bad thing. It depends on the compatibility of cultural and genetic factors. A girl from a different cultural background, say a South Indian girl coming to a Punjabi home, will have difficulty adjusting to the cultural environment. Just as there is cultural maladjustment, there will also be genetic maladjustment. Vedic science has elaborate systems for working this out and it should be calculated either on the basis of books or by a thorough scientific investigation. In India, there are at least eighty systems of marriage, each tribe having their own system and set of rules. These systems should be studied properly before attempting to understand and match the cultural and genetic factors outside of India.

CHILD MARRIAGES

Very young girls are given in marriage. They do not even know their own names, but the village chief pushes them to come forward. What do little girls of twelve or thirteen years old understand? They are given in marriage at such an early age. I am not against marriage. My position is that before marriage a girl should be allowed to pursue her studies, and then choose her own profession. Once she starts earning her living, she will have self-respect and be self-supporting. After that, she may marry at the age of twenty-five to thirty years, if she needs to at all. If she does not feel like marrying, then we are there to take care of such women as sannyasins.

My approach is not to interfere in another's system, because I do not want to become a reformer. A reformer is one who interferes. I do not interfere; rather, I suggest. Nevertheless, circumstances in low caste areas are such that they have to give girls in marriage at an early age, otherwise there are a lot of complications. Anything can happen in their family. Lower caste people are very insecure, so they

marry off their daughters at an early age and send them to the bridegroom's place. However, in the two years since I have been giving bridal kits, we have witnessed the scene change.

Previously, girls of ten and thirteen years were present here to receive their good luck kits from me at Sita Kalyanam. Now those who come are grownup girls of eighteen or twenty years, as I have been insisting, "No marriage at that age." Now there are a few young ones, but the percentage has changed. We suggest there should only be marriage when the girl is suitable for marriage. Why will you marry her off uselessly? Give her in marriage after she is seventeen or eighteen years of age, when she becomes more mature and some understanding develops, and when the boy starts earning.

In India, we now have a law banning child marriages, just to show off to the world that we have a law on this matter.

Even in our homes we have rules because of the pressure from our neighbours. Nevertheless, families and societies do not run by rules. Families and societies thrive only when their foundations are strong. The foundation of any society is its spirituality. It may be in the form of the Koran, the Bible or the *Ramayana*. Whatever form spirituality adopts should be the basis of society. It is only by reading such books that people appreciate and accept spiritual values. A nation should be secular, but it should not condemn or criticize different religions or religious customs.

9

Prasad

PRASAD IS HAPPINESS

Prasad means that which is offered to God. Prasad is from the hands of the Almighty Lord. Prasad means happiness, delight and joy. It is the reverse of pain and sorrow. *Vishad* means unhappiness, dejection and despair. Both prasad and vishad are Sanskrit words. Prasad does not mean presents or gifts, prasad means happiness. That which causes elation in your heart, which makes you very happy, is called prasad. Devi gives you happiness in the form of a lehenga and choli, in the form of a dhoti and a sari. What we get in the temples is prasad and we are very glad to receive it because we desire gifts from the gods and goddesses. Similarly, all the people living around me are working class people, daily wage earners who lift stones on their heads, use portable shops and ride cycles, and they are very happy to receive gifts from Sri Rama. So, this year I have decided to give away twenty-five or thirty portable pushcart shops to these neighbours.

During the four days of the yajna, prasad will be distributed to all the participants in this yajna. We will first offer gifts to the local people who come from the villages in my circle, Rikhia panchayat, as they are our distinguished guests. Rikhia has a population of about ten thousand people, and over a thousand families from five villages are participating in this prasad distribution, as well various other

groups. We honour the village folk first, then the elderly people and then the widows. Next, it will be the turn of the revenue officials of the survey and settlement wing of the state government working in this area. Lastly, the sannyasins will be honoured. Each day of this yajna, with the first chanting of the mantra, we start the distribution.

Whatever you people give me, I distribute. Whatever you give me, you give for others. I am just a postman who delivers letters and money orders to the persons concerned. I am here to deliver God's money orders. That makes me feel very good. I feel so good that I have been employed by the *paramatma*, the great one, who is the creator of this world, controller of the cosmos and the father of all living beings. If you were given this service, would you do it? No, you would rather serve your family and look after your children. If I had wanted to do that, I would have done it a long time ago. If you have to serve somebody, then choose a person who is very wealthy and powerful.

Prasad should be taken as a blessing and not like something you select from a shop. A blessing like this should be received with reverence. There is another point you need to understand related to the distribution of prasad. You may have seen monsoon clouds emanating from the sea. Rain falls upon the earth when these clouds are condensed. This rainwater moves to the ocean through rivers and streams and the same process is repeated. The distribution of prasad is like that. The prasad I have distributed were the offerings made by you to the Divine Mother. So, your offerings and Mother Goddess' grace are being distributed. Those who will distribute the prasad are blessed ones. To give prasad is a meritorious act and to offer prasad is a person's first religious obligation.

BHOLENATH'S GRACE

I knew that Bholenath had been inherited by some benign soul with compassion, with feelings of mercy, with the feeling of atmabhava for all.

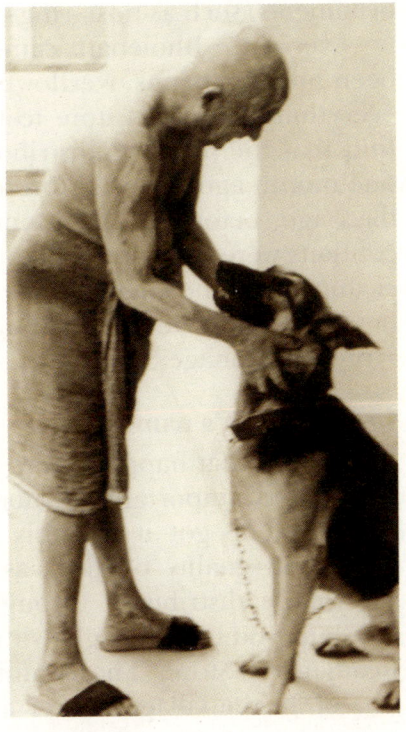

In our Akhara two spirits are very important: one is Tulsi and the other is Bhole. His astrological chart says that he was born under the zodiac sign of *Dhanu*, Sagittarius. Bhole is not the name of my son; it is the name of my dog. He came here at the time when I was performing my panchagni sadhana. Do not get it mixed up. He has had a lot of wealth in his possession right from birth. The people in the neighbouring villages respect him very much and they send prasad for him whenever there is a pooja at their place. They call out to

Bholenath from the street, but nobody dares to come closer. If you can meet him, you will see that he is a very strong, beautiful and intelligent dog. Dogs are always intelligent. They are the combination of two opposite qualities: very affectionate and very ferocious; very greedy and very contented. All dogs are like that.

Bholenath has the blessing of Lakshmi, the goddess of wealth, and if he had been a boy instead of a dog, he would have brought riches and opulence to his home. 'Bholenath's Readymade Store' is the name I have given to the store where we keep prasad for the people of Rikhia. It is a store which is always full of clothes, utensils, tennis racquets, cycles, cows and bulls. There are many toys and games for children such as ludo, snakes and ladders, and for the bigger kids, footballs and cricket bats and balls. For the girls we have a *suhaag*, auspicious, corner. People have now begun giving ornaments, such as nose-rings and earrings.

Ever since Bholenath came here, this prasad store has been full; it remains overflowing all the time. We distribute everything from this store to my neighbours. However, we find that the more we distribute, the more it is filled! Just one month ago and the storeroom was full to the roof. Ten days ago, before the beginning of Sat Chandi, the entire contents were distributed amongst Rikhia panchayat. It was cleaned out. Then, again, over the last eight days that room has been totally filled. Anything anybody wants, Bholenath's Store can manage to give it!

In Bholenath's name

Everything that happens here is in Bholenath's name. Last year a very important Member of Parliament came here. Suddenly, he got it into his head to send five hundred very good quality blankets as an offering for Bholenath! They were distributed throughout the villages. Whatever dakshina you have brought with you will go to the Bholenath Readymade Store. The swamis are now making detailed lists of all the villages. After a few days, the trucks will be loaded with bundles of prasad and everything will be given to the villagers systematically, in the presence of the village chief. All the villagers know that it is Bholenath's prasad. You see, when someone is lucky, you must use him. I found Bholenath was very lucky, so I consecrated everything to him. You should always consecrate your things to someone who is lucky.

Bholenath eats food from only one shop in Deoghar. If you purchase meat elsewhere, he will leave it, because before eating he first smells it. A Muslim family prepares meat for him. They are his bhaktas. Their shop had stopped doing business, but after they started supplying food to Bhole, the family became prosperous. Their shop has expanded and there is a rush of customers. His eldest son could start a teashop. His second son got a rickshaw. They told me, "Swamiji, we now have God's grace in our house and it is all Bholenath's kripa." The wife calls Bhole her good fortune, her lucky star. Whenever she comes here with a full pot of meat, she salutes him and says, "Jai Bholenath." She comes to have his darshan, but Bhole gives darshan to nobody.

A benign soul

Bholenath was not just a dog, he was a spirit incarnate in the body of a dog, and had come for a special purpose. There was absolute poverty here. My neighbours had nothing; nothing in its truest sense. The elders here had maybe one-and-a-half dhotis, which they would wash at night and wear again in the morning. Throughout this entire region, there were houses where the fire in the kitchen would not burn for three or four days because there was nothing for them to cook. Most people have no idea of these intense pangs of hunger.

I had no idea. It was my dog Bholenath who told me. He could communicate with me. His body was that of a dog, just as you have the body of a human being, but some invisible soul had inherited him after he came here. I am not a dog

lover. I do not like dogs at all. I like that adage of Rajneesh's: "Dogs and politicians not permitted here." Somehow things transpired in such a way that he had to stay here. Even though I did not like dogs and I still don't, he stayed. An invisible helper, an invisible soul, inherited him. In 1990, on 14th January, Makar Sankranti, I started my panchagni sadhana. Six months later, I heard a clear voice, a clear mandate about this.

That day Bholenath hinted to me many, many times, "You have a hut, these people have nothing. You have blankets, they have nothing. You eat once a day because that is all you need. However, there are children in some homes who also eat only once, but who need food twice or thrice a day. A child needs milk, and this and that." I knew that Bholenath had been inherited by some benign soul with compassion, with feelings of mercy, with the feeling of atmabhava for all. Everybody experiences his own pain. God alone feels the pain of others, not humans. God experiences the pain of every home. This was the kind of soul Bholenath inherited.

PRASAD DISTRIBUTION

On the holy occasion of this yajna, we have resolved to distribute prasad to the rural people, to the families of Rikhia, to the elderly, to the widows, to the children and to the Santhalis – to honour all who have been associated with this Akhara since its inception and who have cooperated unfailingly with us in all our efforts over the past ten to twelve years.

After coming to Rikhia, a metamorphosis took place in my personality, way of life and destiny. I changed my teaching and my way of thinking. I started distributing prasad at the end of the year to rickshaw drivers, thela drivers, labourers and beggars. My pooja begins from Makar Sankranti, 14th January, to Karka Sankranti, 16th July, when the sun crosses two important points in the heavens. Then until Kartika Poornima I have another program of pooja.

On Kartika Poornima, when both of my anushthanas are over, I offer prasad to the Lord. That prasad is neither fruit nor sweets, neither bael leaves nor tulsi leaves. I make offerings of thousands of items: buckets, cooking pots and utensils for every village home; clothing and jewellery for women; sweaters, toys, slates, pencils, rubbers, sharpeners and comics like *Amar Chitra Katha* for the children; and farming tools, rickshaws and thelas for the strong young men, and autorickshaws for the educated men. Have you noticed that almost all the rickshaws in Deoghar bear the inscription 'Presented by Sivananda Math'? We do not merely offer sweets, flowers and incense as prasad. We prefer to offer something that will be useful to the whole family in the long run.

Marga Sheersha is the best month of the year and we choose it for distributing the prasad. This auspicious month has just started, and during the last three or four days we have started distributing bundles of prasad from village to village. The swamis visit the villages well before the distributions to survey and assess the villagers' requirements. Those who wish to can accompany the swamis when there are distributions in the nearby villages. Please remember that this is not prasad from Swami Satyananda; it is prasad from the Lord, Sri Rama.

Swami Niranjan has just come back from Europe today. He has brought the message of animal donations. Swami Janakananda who came from Denmark said, "I shall give a cow." Denmark is a land of dairy cows, so he has offered to donate a cow. Village people need domesticated animals. They keep sheep, not for food, but for wool. They keep hens for eggs. So, I have received this suggestion from them, that I should give animal donations also, and it is a very good thing. This is a vedic tradition.

Everyone who stays here, even for a day or two, has to help in preparing, stitching, ironing, folding and packing the clothes and other prasad items. The packets are labelled so that people get their exact size. This is necessary as these clothes come in huge quantities from all over India and abroad. An entire building is being used for their storage and distribution. As this inspiration has come from Bholenath, the first distributions are made in his name. Each year in the month of Paush, lists containing details of every family are updated in consultation with the village chief. Every house has a number, and all the details about each family, caste and so on, are entered into the computer. With this information we make the list of beneficiaries.

Prasad from a rajarishi

I am a rajarishi. A rajarishi is somebody who has lived like a *raja*, a king, and also like a rishi. A raja, a king, symbolizes wealth and shakti, power, which are the positive qualities of a king; *jnana*, or knowledge, is the quality of a rishi. A rishi has inner knowledge; he sees the inner light and hears the inner voice. A person who is a rajarishi has these qualities. There are rajarishis, devarishis and brahmarishis, and different types of rishis give different prasad.

When I sit in front of Raghunathji to do my pooja, I feel ashamed to offer Him a mere *batasha*, a sweet. After all, my Lord is not a fakir. He is an emperor, Samrat Chakravarti. How can you offer a sesame seed to an elephant? Lord Rama may not be a god for you, but you will at least accept that he is the king and emperor of Ayodhya. He is a regal person to whom a paltry prasad like batasha or a betel nut simply cannot be offered! So I said, "No, as a rajarishi, let me make

out a list of the royal offerings to be made to the regal hero, like twenty rickshaws, ten ladies' cycles, sixteen spades, forty saris, twenty dhotis, ten pairs of jeans . . ." In this way I go on in my mind, making an offering to the Lord.

At first I was a bit nervous and worried as to how and from where I could get these offerings, especially since I am now totally disconnected from Munger, economically, financially and constitutionally. I am an Alakh Niranjan man. Yes, that disciple is dear to me. He comes and connects Munger with me through his resources. Otherwise, I am not a grandfather enjoying rights over the earnings of the grandchildren until the end of his life. One day I made a list with great hesitation, and the same evening a telephone call came offering a cow and many other items for prasad. By evening everything was arranged.

Honouring different groups
We do not call this prasad 'donation' or 'alms'. We call it honour. We have deleted the words donation and alms from our dictionary. Today we give to the construction workers who have worked ceaselessly for twelve long years to build this ashram. The chief of this group is Yunus Mian Ansari, a Muslim gentleman. He is totally illiterate and does not know how to do accounting, so we do it all for him. He is the actual builder of this Akhara. His masons are all 'Mianjis', very good builders; they work fast. You see, people who build palaces, houses and homes live in huts and slums! They are the builders, the architects of the comforts which all of you enjoy, but they have no facilities to provide themselves with a proper dwelling. These people, the labourers, the workers and the masons who have built this entire Alakh Bara campus, will be given prasad of clothing and accessories, of shoes and blankets, implements and tools of construction.

The Santhalis have done all the construction work here for the past twelve years. They are very honest and hardworking labourers, but very independent. Their character is more European or western than Indian. Indian labourers indulge in pilfering and smoke bidis during working hours. They are shirkers too, but the Santhalis do not shirk work. Because of their character, their quality of work is superior. They have built this big hall and all the other buildings too, as well as digging wells and all types of other work. Their work is very neat and clean. We never have to worry whether or not they will turn up when required. If coal arrives from Dhanbad at night they come to unload it. That is why we hold them in high esteem. It is essential for us to receive all of these workers, to welcome them and to honour them.

Swami Satsangi knows all the builders by heart and they know her by heart. Sometimes she regales them with such piercing orders, "Do you want to work or not? If you do not want to work then go away. We have not engaged you to give away forty rupees every day." The whole day they argue and counter-argue so loudly. She is well-known throughout this area.

Another group which receives prasad are the womenfolk of this area who are known as 'sakhis'. These *sakhis* are actually the companions of Sita during the time of marriage, her attendants. They are given clothes, cosmetics and jewellery, everything that you would wear when you go to a party. You will see the transformation that takes place in them between today and the last day. They look divine and they walk gracefully, they sing joyously and it is a sight to behold.

Gifts of cricket sets will be given to the captains of the Rikhia cricket team and the young people of this area who love to enjoy life, who love to play. I give them a cricket set every year. I hope they will choose their heroes well: Sachin Tendulkar, Ganguli, and so on. Look at our children, the little girls from the village. Girls who sing well are also given tape recorders and cassettes. There is nothing in it for me. I ask the people to give, and the things which they offer are distributed. As a sannyasin, I have to beg, but why beg for myself? I have begged for two rotis and two langotis for myself, but for others, I can ask for anything.

Giving and receiving

Do not feel that I obtain all these things by magic. It is not like the deeds of some siddhas or adepts who could manifest butter oil from air or water! You have made all the offerings. These are your gifts that are now being distributed as prasad; whatever is offered to you should be accepted as divine grace. You offer to Devi, and I offer it back as Devi's prasad. Just as sweets that you present to the deity in a temple are given back to you as prasad, you present your offerings to the Divine Mother and the Divine Mother gives you Her prasad in return.

In the tradition followed in the Rajasooya Yajna, there are three essential aspects. The first is worship of the deity, which means sitting and singing the praises of God, doing kirtan or listening to the glorious exploits of godheads. The second includes the ritualistic installation, the chanting of mantras and so on. The third is giving and receiving. The yajna cannot be complete without daan, giving. This was the tradition when Sri Rama ruled the earth. The tradition was followed during the Dwapara period and the same tradition should also be followed during the present age, Kali Yuga. In Kali Yuga, however, the pandits have deviated from the tradition and instead of giving they have become used to taking. The brahmins and pandits receive things in the form of dakshina. They form societies and associations and collect some forty to fifty thousand rupees, spend a part of the huge collection on performing the yajna and save the rest for their own use.

I keep asking God, "God why have you forgotten these innocent, pious, clean-hearted, poor villagers? They are foremost in discharging their religious duties, foremost in manual labour and you have forgotten them?" Seventy percent of India is totally ignored and I make this statement on the golden jubilee celebration of your freedom and independence. These people live only by the name of God; only God sustains them. They enjoy no amenities, no privileges from the nation. This nation has not even given them drinking water. The nation has given them no facilities whatsoever. Whatever funds the nation spends are directed towards big cities like Delhi, Mumbai, Bangalore and Kanpur. No money comes into the villages. In the Kali Yuga there are only two paths for achieving one's ultimate goal: one is God's name, *naam*, and the other is giving, *daan*. Therefore, it is not social service that I am doing for them, it is prasad distribution.

A variety of offerings
Clothes, *vastra daan*, are offered in the first year of a Rajasooya Yajna, and in the second year utensils and vessels are offered, *patra daan*. So forget about clothes when you come next year. You will be given spoons, pots, thalis, water pots and the like which can be used for eating or in your kitchen. We will offer all the types of utensils that you find in the world.

During the third year of the yajna, it is mandatory to offer cooked food and grains as prasad. If it is not done in the third year, then it will be done in the fifth year. If it is not done by the fourth or fifth year, then the yajna is considered to be a failure, it becomes null and void. For five days the ashram will feed everybody in and around Rikhia. There will be poori, halwa, laddoos and so forth, and if you bring your cows, bullocks, buffaloes, goats, pigs, and hens, fodder will be provided for them too, during those five days. From sunrise to sunset thousands of people will partake of the food we offer. This offering of food is called *anna daan*. It is the most difficult part of the yajna. Swami Niranjan told me that he could manage it this year, but I declined because there is a sequence to all these things.

Offering of knowledge is of very great importance, greater than the offering of food. Knowledge will be offered in the twelfth year and, God willing, if my mood is conducive, you may have the bliss of shaktipat from me too. One day you will get gold and silver as prasad. It is not a big thing. It is you who offer it all. Yes, you are the donors. Some of you may get diamond rings, some gold. We may cover one thousand, ten thousand, twenty thousand, thirty thousand people. Everyone here will receive prasad because you are the people who contribute to it. From the yajna onwards, tractor-loads of prasad will go from village to village and each family will receive prasad, in every nook and corner of Rikhia panchayat. All the people of Deoghar district will also receive prasad.

As is the practice, when kings and emperors come to attend the Rajasooya Yajna they offer diamonds, gold, emeralds, sapphires, pearls, and so on, to the *chakravarti samrat,* the great monarch, and the monarch distributes it as prasad to the people. The chakravarti receives it as a gift or offering and gives it away as the prasad of the yajna. In ancient times the Rajasooya Yajna was performed on a very large scale. We are following the same tradition. Even today many yajnas are held in this country, compared to which this is a miniature yajna. But this is a prelude to a very major event. We believe in that rich tradition. My Indian guests and disciples must keep that in mind.

The divine power which is invoked here through yajna, mantra and God's name has the potential to fulfil the desire of every human being. So, you will surely feel good because this is happening for everyone's good.

Karmic debt to society

When I came to Rikhia many things became clear to me, the foremost of which was that I am not to participate in marriages or funerals. It is the vow of a sannyasin, because marriage and funeral are both taboo for a sannyasin. As I could not participate in their marriages, I decided to give these girls gold on the occasion of dwiragaman, and the reason behind it is this. You may not be aware that it is the girls who have contributed most to the cause of yoga and yajna. It is their diligence and dedication that has been uppermost. So when I came here I thought that my first and foremost duty was towards the girls.

When the daughter goes back to her husband's house after marriage, he gives her beautiful clothes and finery. If she stands in finery in front of you, imagine she is your own daughter. Who knows, she might come as your daughter in your next life, so it is better that you deal with her now. That way, you exhaust the karmas of your future births also. Everybody has to bear the fruit of karma. In the *Ramacharitamanas* it has very aptly been said:

The Lord bestows fruits
According to a man's
Good or evil karmas.
A man receives fruits
According to his own deeds.
The Vedas, the scriptures
And all people say so.

The *Bhagavad Gita* has also said (4:40): "The ignorant, the faithless, the doubting self goes to destruction; there is neither this world nor the other, nor happiness for the doubting." Just as you marry off your own daughter, we also help a girl to get married and send her off to her husband. The bonds of karma carry forward from lifetime to lifetime. If we get two to three thousand girls married and sent away to live with their husbands, then we have offloaded so many lifetimes of karmic debt. This is the spirit.

You are indebted to the society in which you live, which is all around you. If you do not redeem that debt, then you become a culprit of the disorder that will creep into the society in which you exist. You owe a debt to the society you live in and you must discharge that debt. If there was no society then you would be living in a jungle. Today you are secure because you are part of an organized society. If you destroy that society, you will not survive. Remember this; you have an organized society for your own security. Society is your security and you are a part of that society. Therefore, you cannot ignore the debt you have to pay.

The proper recipient

There is no need for you to go to the villages. Whatever you wish to donate can be done through an institution. If you give charity and assistance to the poor in the cities, it will only increase the congestion and make the city dirtier, because if the migrants and others get free assistance they will continue to stay on there. Therefore, assistance and charity should be directed towards the villages. Villages all over the world are like pregnant women, while the cities and

towns are like barren women. If rapid urbanization stops, crime, poverty, filth and slums can be eradicated. In order to achieve this, help must reach the villages.

In the *Bhagavad Gita* we find the description of three types of gifts (17:20–22):

> The gift which is given to one who does nothing in return, knowing it to be a duty to give in a fit place and time to a worthy person, is held to be sattwic. The gift which is given with a view to receiving something in return, or looking for a reward, or reluctantly, is held to be rajasic. The gift that is given at a wrong place and time, to unworthy persons, without respect or with insult, is declared to be tamasic.

PRASAD: SYMBOL OF GOD'S GRACE

This prasad is given to you in the name of God, so accept what you are receiving with joy. Prasad is not of different gods. God is one and He is in your heart, in your head, in everyone's heart.

When you do pooja you offer something to God, some sweets, laddoos and sugar candies. When you go to a temple and offer something, what does the priest do? He gives you a sweet as prasad and you take it. Similarly, what we are giving is not charity. We are making an offering in God's name and then distributing it as prasad.

According to my faith and philosophy, whatever is given to others is given as prasad from God. This is not social service or charity; it is nothing philanthropic. There should be no ego in it. To think, 'I am doing social service for humanity' is nothing but ego. Who am I? It is God who does it. If people give me fifty blankets, I give them to the Lord. What is meant by offering something to God? You must go to the temple and dedicate it to the Lord. It is a *sankalpa*, a resolve. When you feel love, devotion and affection for someone, then whatever you think about that person becomes your pooja, your worship, your sankalpa.

It is God who helps

When you give, the attitude should not be one of giving charity. Our feeling regarding such affairs has to be spontaneously spiritual, not intellectually spiritual. How do I help my own brother? If my wife is sick, what do I do for her? If my father is sick, what do I do for him? I do not give charity to my father. If my mother or child is sick, do I give them charity? No, I give them my love, my feelings, my support. I do my duty towards them because I feel as one with them. There is a feeling of unity on an emotional plane or a spiritual plane. The level at which you feel unity depends upon your evolution. Actually, it is God who helps people. If somebody has to be helped somewhere in any part of the world through you, me or somebody else, it is He who is helping; I am only the medium.

That is the basic philosophy upon which this *Rama Naam Aradhana* is based. At the end of the worship, prasad has to be given because there can be no worship without prasad. You cannot worship with empty hands. You cannot send people back empty-handed. This is the philosophy of my life. Why? Because God gave me this wisdom. I do not care for samadhi myself. I only want to be able to remove the pain and misery of the helpless. It needs God's special power to remove the woes of suffering humanity, to wipe away the tears of crying people. It is a spiritual power, not an ordinary power, which enables one to alleviate human sorrow. If you really want to help people, you need a special power from God.

A man came recently and gave five thousand blankets. What can I do with five thousand blankets; put them on myself? These blankets go to five thousand people as prasad. This will give them happiness because they need it. These Yugoslavian girls are weaving hundreds of sweaters here in Rikhia and also in Munger. Now they have also brought in machines to speed up the weaving. I have told them to weave sweaters for small children, aged four to seven, who must have sweaters to protect them from the cold winter weather. Gifts for the village people are coming in from all directions.

The Rotary Club, the Lions Club, the devotees are all sending truckloads of things. There is one group from South America and another large group from Greece arriving with enormous suitcases of gifts. Just a while ago, a group went to the bazaar in Deoghar and emptied the shops with their buying sprees. They bought all the utensils in one of the shops. Every one of these items will be offered to the Lord in the daily pooja. It then becomes prasad which we load into the trucks and take for distribution to the village families. So, when you take that truck into the villages and give them the prasad, you should never think that you are doing charity or social service. That is a completely materialistic idea. It is not a good idea and does not come to me at all. It is the prasad of Lord Rama.

The recipients are also given to understand that it is not social service or charity, but prasad. Nobody should call it a donation or charity. This distribution of prasad has been going on for many years, but I do not take anything from Bihar School of Yoga. I do not want any institution to be my benefactor. God is my benefactor. If He gives me something, I will give it to you. If He does not give me anything, then I will not because He does not want me to. So, I put the prasad list before Him and in this way we started giving.

Symbol of God's grace

God gives to me and tells me what to do. He has told me that this year I will have to give a token of prasad, a token of grace. It may be a *tabiz*, an amulet, which will be symbolic of God's grace. If I offer you a pashmina shawl, do not feel that it is from me. Swami Satyananda does not have that capacity, because everything in the world is His property. So if you receive a pashmina shawl from me, then you should know that you have received a symbol of God's grace, although it has come to you through me. It is not an offering or a selfless act or righteousness on my part. It is only God's grace, which you may get in any form. You are, however, at liberty to beg from God directly. There is no objection to that, but my duty is to give this prasad to you.

PRACTICAL GIFTS

Many visitors have asked about the type of gifts they should donate for distribution to the village people. Whatever you give should be practical, something that is useful not to rich people, but to poor people. What does a poor man need? He does not need a candle; he needs a lantern. He does not need a little idol of Ganesha; he needs a bottle of kerosene oil. The gifts of the yajna have to be practical because they are given to the poor people around us who do not have much. When people give very fancy gifts, I tell them that I will have to give them to those who have a lot of money. I give walkie-talkies to rich people who come from Deoghar or Pune. Some of you will be getting one; they are of no use here for my neighbours. What will these poor people do with a walkie-talkie?

In yajna, the significance of a gift is that it is for the ordinary person. Rich people do not need a gift at all; they should be givers rather than receivers. Therefore, you have to ask me exactly what type of gift needs to be given. Your gift is not just to please someone. Your gift is not just to pass on your emotion to someone. The gifts should have some practical purpose, to help a person in need, whether it is a blanket, a pashmina shawl, a pair of shoes, an umbrella, a hurricane lantern, a satchel for a school child, a compass or a pencil case. I have lists of items to be given. Do not purchase anything else. Otherwise you will bring sweets like barfi and sandesh. A man does not live by barfi and sandesh.

Anna Daanam

The fire ceremony which the pandits are conducting marks the successful culmination of this Sat Chandi Mahayajna. This time (2002) the prasad of the yajna was *patra*, utensils and containers. People came from all over the world and donated different kinds of containers. Now, the local people have all the vessels and containers they need in their kitchens. They have received such an abundance of containers over the last few days that they find their kitchens too small to contain them all. Next year the prasad will be *anna daanam*, the five traditional grains: wheat, rice, millet, maize and barley, which will be offered to Devi. By anna, food grains, we live. So, all the local people, as well as the participants of the yajna, will receive grains in abundance next year as the prasad of the yajna.

I expect to receive grain from everyone next year, not flowers, not chocolates, not greeting cards. Our ancestors spoke of five grains: wheat, rice, gram, maize and mustard. These are the five foods which are most important for the survival of human beings. Flowers and greeting cards do not feed the hungry stomach. Hunger and starvation exist, not only in India, but everywhere. In every corner of the world, there are hungry souls whose children sleep without a morsel of food. In Africa, Asia, South America and even Europe and North America, there are people who need food for survival. Therefore, I say, "Feed man and God will be fed." If man dies hungry, God will also die because the existence of God depends on man.

I have lived amongst the poor all my life and my habits are like any poor man in India. Even if I wanted to live like the rich, I could not because I have lived with the poor and developed their habits. You may not have seen or heard about the poor, but I have seen and I have lived with them. Even now, I live amongst them; they are all around me. So this is a very important injunction to every spiritual aspirant and to all of you. Next year, do not bring candles. Candles are good inside churches and temples, flowers are good when you want to meet your boyfriend or girlfriend, and greeting cards are good when you want to do business. However, grain is necessary to feed the hungry stomach and, at the same time, it is necessary to maintain the law and order of the universe: *annad bhavanti bhutani*. This important truth is conveyed in the *Taittiriya Upanishad* and in the *Bhagavad Gita* as well.

Definite needs

A poor man has certain definite needs in life, especially in this country. You know that very well, and if you don't, I'm just making it very clear to you. The people here do not need the things you desire. What is the use of a transistor or even a television set? Make gifts of cows and bulls, cycle rickshaws, sewing machines, utensils for cooking and containers for storing, drinking and serving. Give saris, towels, dhotis, cloth to make shirts and pants, and of course, grains: rice, pulse, barley, wheat, and so on. Bring shoes and blankets, implements and tools of construction. These are useful gifts to alleviate suffering and to fulfil some of their needs.

This year someone has also sent good pairs of shoes. I am wearing a pair and they are quite comfortable. The remaining pairs I will present to my sons-in-law. Someone else has presented umbrellas. They will now use umbrellas and raincoats, and next year I will give them gumboots. In China, Thailand and Japan I have seen women wearing gumboots while working in the fields during the rainy season. Here, the female labourers stand in mud and water for six or seven hours at a time when they work in the fields transplanting rice. Some develop sores on their feet, so it will be good to provide them with gumboots.

Gifts have to be offered pragmatically. One of my disciples brought a microwave oven, which I declined because I do not need such things personally, and these rural folk whose welfare is supreme to me, cannot use it. So I did not accept it. In the same manner one disciple brought a gas oven. However, poor village folk cannot use it, as a gas cylinder for the oven would cost more than two hundred and fifty rupees per week. A poor man hardly gets forty rupees a day. With that he has to have his daughter married and look after his medical bills. Therefore, please do not bring anything of your own choice, but find out from me what needs to be given. Do not do it for your own pleasure.

I collect diaries and distribute them to boys and girls who go to school; otherwise, they have to buy notebooks from the store. The cost is twelve rupees each and they find that difficult to afford. Their exams are drawing near and soon they will start their next term. Therefore, we bought paper from Patna and had it ruled and bound into notebooks which cost only two rupees each. I had twenty thousand notebooks made through Swami Niranjan and we will be able to give five notebooks each to the schoolchildren.

When I started giving walkmans to village children they asked me what they should listen to. I told them it is up to them, whatever they like. One day when Tripura was wearing earphones at the building site, a villager thought it was a hearing aid. It was then I realized that if children in the cities can have personal tape recorders to listen to music, why not the children from the villages? This year is the golden jubilee of Indian independence, so giving the children this special gift is expected of us.

COWS FOR THE RURAL PEOPLE

Today we are presenting the first cow, which has been donated by Swami Janakananda, a very senior disciple from Denmark. Denmark is a country where a lot of milk is available and they love cows. They do not consider them as their mothers as we do in India, but they do look after them correctly. There, milk and butter flow like rivers, and the people eat lots of cheese and drink lots of milk. One day Swami Janakananda telephoned to say that he wanted to donate a cow. It was a wonderful idea. I said, "Okay, we will make a new program, for there is no better gift in the whole world than a cow."

The greatest gift

A cow is the greatest gift that you can give, whether for a birthday, for Christmas or for any other reason, whether you consider the cow to be holy, or useful, or whatever. This year we will give cows to the local farmers. This is one asset a farmer ought to have. The people here are not white collar office workers; they are all very poor labourers. Some are Hindu, some Muslim. The entire Rikhia panchayat could be labelled as a 'backward community'. In the *Mahabharata*, Bhishma explains the importance of cows to Yudhishthira:

> *Cow, earth and Saraswati have similar qualities.*
> *These three should be offered to others.*
> *The result of gifting anyone of them is the same.*
> *These three fulfil the desires of man.*
> *The cow is the mother of living beings,*
> *And capable of giving happiness to all.*
> *One who desires upliftment*
> *Should circumambulate the cow from the right side.*

It has also been said in *Vrihatparashara Smriti*:

> *Even by touching cows, all the sins of man are destroyed.*
> *If served with respect, they bestow affluence.*
> *If given as gifts, they take one to the heavens.*
> *There is no wealth comparable to them.*

For an Indian farmer, a cow is a must. All the household devis and devatas reside in the cow. Wherever there is a cow, the air becomes pure. Even the waste or excretory matter of the cow is pure. Imagine the purity of an animal whose excretory matter is pure and free of germs, and kills germs.

Cow dung produces a combustible gas called *gobar* gas, which can be burnt in lamps to give light. This process also produces high quality manure. Gobar gas can be used for cooking by connecting the line to a gas stove. Two cows are sufficient to meet a family's gas requirements for cooking. There is no need for firewood; cow dung is the only fuel required. Even gas cylinders are not needed. Even if a cow is barren or old and does not give milk, she will be able to cut the cost of fire wood. It has been mentioned in the *Vishnu Purana*:

> *That place where cows live becomes pure.*
> *That house where cows are kept becomes pure.*
> *It is said that by smearing the floor of a place*
> *With cow dung, it becomes pure.*
> *Yajnashalas and temples should be smeared with cow dung.*
> *In cow dung, Lakshmi herself resides always.*

This morning, Swami Janakananda went to purchase a cow. The cost of a cow depends on how much milk she gives and whether it is her first or second calf. He did this through a veterinarian who knows all the cows, so that we do not get duped. The cow he bought produces four litres of milk. When the chosen family receives the cow, the children will get milk, which is a complete food. If you have milk, you do not need roti, rice and sabji. There is only one tattwa which cow's milk does not contain, which goat's milk does. When you mix cow's milk and goat's milk together, then you do not need meat, eggs, roti or dal. If a family has a cow which gives four litres of milk, they are self-sufficient. Milk is a sattwic food which is good for everybody: children, mothers, pregnant women, sick or healthy people, weight lifters or athletes. I thank Swami Janakananda for this brilliant idea.

Donation of cows

The village people are the ones who know how to maintain cows. Cows are a part of their lives. The urban population only know how to drink milk and have forgotten how to keep cows. They should send their cows here. We will look after them well and they will be repaid in the form of blessings. The cows kept by the village people are of the local strain, not breeds from Punjab and Haryana. Even Jersey cows are not in demand here because the bulls that they produce are neuters. There are many factors to consider and Swami Satsangi knows about this.

The Marwari community attaches a lot of importance to the donation of cows. A local Marwari helps to transport cows here from Gaya by truck. Then cows are examined by our vet and thoroughly checked for disease. Swami Satsangi then speaks to the head of the village to decide who should receive the cows and to determine whether they can learn to keep a cow properly. Her department is very efficiently organized. She has full details on computer of all the families living in hundreds of villages in this area, which is something even the government does not have.

Some basic facilities are required to look after a cow. They must have a cowshed and the means to provide fodder. Then a member of the family must come here twice a day for one month. They are taught everything, including milking and cleaning, for an hour in the morning. In the course of time, I am also going to introduce a gobar gas plant so that they can create their own fuel for cooking.

Swami Niranjan has also started to give prasad of bulls in this area, and today the first pair of bulls is being given. Gradually, every needy farmer will become recipients of cows or bulls, as these animals are very necessary in this area.

Seva to the animals
Sri Swamiji (To the recipient of the first pair of bulls): "Listen, the way to your house has now been cleared for Lakshmi, the goddess of prosperity. Serve the oxen more than you serve your sons and daughters. Your children will spend your wealth, but these bulls will earn wealth for you. Earning members have joined your family. Care for them as if they were your sons, not animals. Do seva to them every day. Massage their bodies like you massage your father's aching limbs. Serve them and do not ever hit them or twist their tails. Give them beautiful names with love. Ask your wife to graze them well. Work efficiently with them and when your work is done, let them also plough the soil of some other needy people."

A cow produces milk just as human mothers produce milk for their babies, and just as trees produce fruit. A cow has to be carefully looked after. I have a degree in the scientific aspects of keeping cows. I studied all this in my childhood. All of you who have cows, please note that a person who has tuberculosis (TB) should never attend to a cow. Only those people who do not have cough-related problems should attend to a cow. The weakest point of a cow is that it is susceptible to droplet infections and its milk becomes infected.

We are trying to find out which houses have TB patients and how many family members are infected. If all the members of a family are TB patients, we will not give a cow to that family. The cow will definitely contract TB because it is very susceptible to it. Keep this in mind. However, those people who have undergone treatment for tuberculosis and have recovered from it, should have first preference. A list has been made of people suffering from TB in this vicinity. We have selected thirty TB patients for treatment. Some people from Mumbai have taken charge of them. The medicines have already come, and when the doctors come from Bhagalpur in a few days' time, the medication will start. We also currently treat children, pregnant women and young women, and, where necessary, cows will be given to their families so that their families will be able to improve their health. These poor people cannot eat mutton every day, but they will be able to drink milk.

These days, the local cows do not have the capacity that you read of in the scriptures, where they speak about rivers of milk flowing. Many people here hardly even get to see milk, but we will change the picture of the place in the

next few years. If they do not have cereal, they will surely have milk. Last year we donated many cows to the villagers. However, I do not want these people to become rich, because the moment wealth comes, bottles of wine enter the house. Wealth moves people away from their path.

Training in caring for cows
Sri Swamiji: Now for prasad. Please bring the recipient forward. Have you ever kept a cow?

Villager: Yes, a small cow, but she did not give milk.

Sri Swamiji: All right. This cow will give milk as well as a calf. Serve her well. She gives two litres more than they tell you because we keep a person throughout the day to tend her. He massages her neck and her legs. When the cow sees that we are serving her well, she is pleased with us and thinks, 'Oh, these people work so hard for me, I must give them a commission of one litre of milk.' Therefore, fawn upon the cow a little bit, pamper her and Lakshmi will enter your house. However, I have made a condition which you will have to fulfil before you receive a cow. Someone from your family must come here to learn how to look after her. They have to come every morning and evening for one full month to learn about the diseases affecting cows.

Holy cow
One cow that was brought here was declared to be giving ten litres of milk, but actually she gives fifteen. Keeping a cow is not like keeping a goat or a ram and employing a servant to raise it. You must try to look after your cow yourself, and if you cannot do that then at least spend a little time each day caring for her. Why? Because she is your mother and her milk brings abundance to your life. In India, there is the tradition of feeding the cow. Before each meal, the lady of the house will first feed the cow a morsel made up of all the food she has cooked for her family, and then the rest of the family will sit down to eat. The cow is the abode of all deities; all deities dwell in her.

Everything in the world creates waste matter which is poisonous and hazardous to health, be it human, chemical, industrial or nuclear waste. No waste matter in the world is safe except that of the cow. There is only one living being whose stool and urine are edible and drinkable, and that's the cow. All other living beings excrete waste matter that is highly toxic. There are no bacteria, infections or worms in a cow's waste matter that could harm you. In fact, in the villages, the women sweep and polish the floors of their houses with fresh cow dung, every day; it is considered an antiseptic. Therefore, when a cow's waste matter or excreta is so pure, can you imagine how pure and clean that creature must be?

The cow is the most holy of animals; she is called 'holy cow'. For the villagers, two things are important: water and a cow. There would be no poverty or starvation if we just had water and a cow. The government opens schools and colleges, which is useless. People die of starvation, but nobody sends water, nobody installs taps, nobody makes canals, nobody digs tube wells. There are primary health centres and people go there as victims of starvation; they are sick and dying due to hunger. In villages, water and cows are the most essential of necessities. Even if there is no bread, a villager should at least be able to drink cow's milk.

I have seen many mahatmas who have enjoyed a long lifespan stretching to over one hundred years, just by drinking cow's milk. Have you heard the term *dudhahari* mahatmas? It means the 'great ones whose diet is milk only'. Such mahatmas can live to the ripe old age of one hundred. In the *Atharva Veda* it has been said about the cow:

> *The cow is the mother of the twelve Adityas*
> *And the daughter of the eight Vasus.*
> *She is the life of the subjects*
> *And the source of amrit or nectar.*
> *She is the giver of sweet, golden ghee,*
> *By virtue of which great vigour*
> *Circulates in the body of the mortals.*

DARSHAN OF GODDESS LAKSHMI

The goddess of wealth has assured me, "Satyananda, as long as you do not live a life of luxury and selfishness, I will leave this blank cheque with you. Whatever I give to you, give it as prasad to everybody. If you use it for yourself I will go away. You just watch and you will see this happen! After pooja distribute the prasad to everybody in accordance with their needs." I said, "Your order is on my head."

While being in the service of God, I get a chance to have the daily darshan of Goddess Lakshmi and because of Her darshan, I have no need to beg for money. It is not a big thing for me to collect ten thousand, twenty thousand and forty thousand rupees as guru dakshina in a year. It is a very small thing. Daily in the early morning, I clean the room thoroughly before the arrival of Goddess Lakshmi. You know I am her servant. I wash her sari and petticoat, clean her utensils and prepare her food. She gives me something and at the same time does not give me anything. She gives something to others through me. Now our prasad store is full and we will also need all the buildings in the Akhara to store the items for distribution. Soon, the trucks will go out loaded with prasad. The lists of every family in each and every village are ready.

Agreement with Lakshmi

Goddess Lakshmi has warned me not to indulge in any hanky panky, "You have asked for others, haven't you? Whatever is given, it is for others." Therefore, I have an agreement with Lakshmi. It is not a joke, though I say things in a jocular manner. Lakshmi said to me, "I permit you to meet all your needs, but not your desires. Yes, I can grant you a loincloth, a blanket and a candle because these are your needs. But the moment you ask for a fancy object out of desire, I will immediately cancel the blank cheque I have sanctioned for you." When Swami Janakananda came and said, "I shall donate a cow from here," I said, "No, donate it directly from where you purchase it. Don't bring it to me." I am scared that Lakshmiji may take away my privilege. Therefore, serve Lord Narayana, and you will automatically get the grace of Goddess Lakshmi, because she is a *sati pativrata*, devoted to her husband.

Every morning I sit here and hand over the prasad list to Swami Satsangi. So far, Lakshmi has approved all my bills. No bill of mine is pending with her. Lakshmi is in charge of all the wealth in the world. Saraswati is in charge of all the arts and learning. Bhavani is in charge of all the power and energy. I regard Lakshmi as the highest because she is the goddess of Kali Yuga, the present age. Of course, all the goddesses are important. This is exactly how it is and in spite of all this, I know for sure that without God's sanction man cannot even do one good turn. If you and I think that we can do good in the world, then we are wrong in our thinking. At least that's what I think.

Earrings from God

It is God's wish that this year, 2001, the married women of this panchayat will receive two big earrings, or *jhumakas*. A thought process had been going on in my mind as to what to give the womenfolk during Sita Kalyanam. Then, one day I heard a cassette tape being played in an adjoining village. The song was, *"Jhumaka gira re, Bareilly ke bazaar mein."* It is a funny song. It means, "Somebody dropped their earrings in the market of Bareilly." Bareilly is in Uttar Pradesh. I did not understand the meaning so I asked Swami Satsangi what a jhumaka was because I am not familiar with these ornaments. She said that jhumakas were long earrings of silver or gold.

Immediately, I resolved to distribute jhumakas to all the women and girls of this panchayat during Sita's wedding. I thought, "Now God wants me to give earrings to married women. Oh my God! In India there are so many married women! I will have to make a choice. In Rikhia panchayat where I live, there may be two or three thousand married women."

God works through us

Just see how God sends people from unknown quarters to fulfil the desires of His devotees. He works through anyone because He is in everyone's heart. When I decided to give earrings to all the rural women, the idea struck someone living far away from here and he sent an email offering me three thousand pairs of earrings. This is not a small offering; it is a big consignment. This is the first year of the Rajasooya Yajna and we have received this large offering. Maybe in the concluding year of Rajasooya we will receive gold and diamonds. Who can say? Just see how things happen. God resides in your heart, so every one of you will get your prasad.

Give without expectation

One day, one of the villagers came with a complaint: "Swamiji, you gave a cow to that man and he has sold it." He informed Swami Satsangi and she was in a panic: "Oh, we gave him a cow and he has sold it. He is making fools of us. He thinks that we are idiots." I said, "Just be quiet. Don't press the panic button." You know, this younger generation pushes the panic button very fast. I said, "Don't worry." Swami Satsangi was terribly upset. Her ego was hurt. She thought that she had been made a fool of and that people would consider Swami Satyananda a foolish man. I said, "God has given us so many precious things and we have misused them. God knows it, but what does he think?"

God is thinking, and his assistant points out, "You have given so much to this man and look what he is doing there!" God says, "It doesn't matter, he will follow his karma." The moment you act, you create a karma and the moment you create a karma, there is an equal and opposite reaction. So to everyone I give prasad, I say, "I am giving this gift to you and you can sell it if you like, I won't mind in the least. If you can get five hundred, five thousand or ten thousand rupees for your evening meal or even for your bottle or for a girl in the night, I don't mind. The gift is yours. God has given it to you and you are responsible for your karma. I will not be responsible for your karma." Now those who were bringing complaints have stopped coming because they know this swami will not stop giving. He says, "Continue, continue."

Unconditional giving from God

After all, I am a gift of God and I have realized this in my life. My speech, my mind, my life are gifts of God. God has given us so many things, but we have misused them. If we can misuse the things given to us by God, then anybody can misuse the things given to them by me. I am a mere human being. My attitude is very simple. If I give a cycle rickshaw and the recipient sells it and pockets the money, I will not mind. This is the philosophy of God. A social worker expects the person whom he helps to be honest. I do not expect that. I am a realist, not an idealist. Has God put any conditions on what He has given to all of us? No. If we misuse what He has given, does He punish us? No.

True generosity is giving without conditions. Suppose you give someone a blanket worth one hundred and fifty rupees, but he goes to the market and sells it for a mere fifty rupees. Then you feel discouraged and begin to think, 'I gave him a blanket and he sold it. Why did I give it at all?' If you feel like this about a blanket, imagine how it would be if God were to have the same attitude about all the things He has given to you.

We generally have a feeling that people are going to cheat us. Yes, there are people who cheat, but the number of people who think they will be cheated is much greater than the numbers who cheat. So, give! We should not always think that we will be cheated. That destroys our faith and makes us narrow. A person like this is neither a king nor a rishi. The king would say, "What will he take? Only some money." A king or a rishi is not afraid of anybody. So, whenever you help others and do charity, remember that you are doing it for God's sake. Everybody says that service to others is service to the Lord. I am just reminding you of an old truth. Kabir has so aptly remarked:

God never resides in those
Who are full of doubts.
There is not a feather of a doubt
In the minds of those
Who are devotees of Rama.

Everything in me: the goodness, the evil, the intelligence, the idiocy and the genius are all gifts of God. So I will think and behave like Him. I cannot be God, but I can definitely think about how God thinks. Now the whole trend has changed. One man in a village nearby had quietly sold his cow. It now costs five to ten thousand rupees for one cow with a calf. When that man sold his cow, the whole village turned against him. They said, "If you do not bring back the cow, we are going to excommunicate you from the panchayat." Therefore, he had to return the cow. It has become so difficult for the people of this community to misuse my prasad!

Training to give and share

I have involved the kanyas and batuks in distributing prasad to the people gathered here at the Sat Chandi Mahayajna as a means of training. Let the children come forward to learn the basic lesson of giving to others. To give, to donate and to share your bread with your less fortunate brothers and sisters is the loftiest ideal of life. The worst type of meanness and pettiness is to sit tight on your possessions. The most despicable part of human character is to crave everything and not share your wealth with others. Try and learn to give to others. You have not learnt this noble ideal so far. I am not

referring to the children. I am referring to the adults who are very miserly.

The poor, the impoverished and the affluent all participate in the yajna. This time we have put the children in the forefront, because they are the up and coming generation. We will have the prasad distributed from their hands as we wish to banish meanness from our society. By and large, people are very tight-fisted and you know that miserliness is the weakest point in man's character. Therefore, children should learn early in life how to share their pleasure with their fellow beings. They should imitate the habit of giving. Giving good samskaras in the formative years will bring about changes in their attitude to life. I could have had the prasad distributed by any group of people, but I have involved the children in this work for their training. To give or share is an art.

Children should learn how to give, how to share their food and other things with others. Training in receiving is not essential because a child learns this in the mother's womb. I don't give that training, as children are born with it; they are trained graduates in that matter, past masters, so to say. If children are trained in giving and sharing, they will learn how to give when they are grown up.

The society which knows only one culture, the culture of receiving and not giving, promotes social exploitation. To strike a balance in society we should teach children to follow the culture of give and take. Your parents teach you only to receive and take from others. They must teach you to give as well. I am not saying you should only teach them to give. No, that is not my point. If we do not receive from others, how can we give? We should strike a balance between the two and only then can social balance be sustained. Unless this social balance is achieved, the gap between affluence and poverty cannot be bridged.

We should, therefore, train our children to strike a balance between giving and taking. If you earn a lot, you must spend too. If your child earns three thousand rupees a month, he spends two thousand on domestic requirements and puts a thousand into fixed deposit. Ask him to spend a few rupees on others also. If you do not give to others how will you get anything back? If you purchase something from a shop, the transaction is complete only when you have paid. You purchase a utensil from a shop and pay for it. The shopkeeper goes to the market and purchases food and clothing with that earning. This is how society runs and there is a social balance. To keep this element of social balance, provision has been made in the yajna for daan, giving of prasad.

Service to the Lord

I do not care for social work. My guru used to undertake a lot of philanthropic work, but I could not understand what he was up to. He used to feed lepers and clothe scavengers. I could not understand why he did it. Every person has his own personality and temperament. I have a personality and temperament which does not believe in charity. I firmly believe that everyone should fend for themselves, that everyone should live by their own means and not at the mercy of others. One who lives off charity is not fit to live as a human being. I am not doing anything for charity.

You should not think that what we are doing here is social service. This is prasad, not social service. The concept of social service is giving aid at the time of an emergency, when there are natural calamities. Calamity is the mother of poverty. If there is an earthquake and then you help, that is social service. Otherwise, whenever you help others, it should be with the spirit of offering service to the Lord. When God gives the order, His servant works for him. In this way it should be understood that I am not serving society but obeying God.

The *Bhagavad Gita* says (17:24): "Therefore, the followers of the Vedas should undertake acts like yajna, service and austerities as directed by the scriptures, with the recitation of *Om* in the beginning." If a sadhu comes to your house and you are well-off, it is your duty to give him some food. However, do not give with that spirit; give as an offering. If a beggar comes

to your house, do not have the attitude of helping a poor man. Instead, feel that you are giving to the Lord. Who knows? Lord Narayana can come in any form. Kabir says:

In this world one should meet
With others without reservation
Because who knows in which form
Narayana might appear

The ultimate philosophy
When you help others, you are helping yourself. Do not think about yourself so much. You think too much about yourself, your children, your husband, your boyfriend. Think about them a little bit. A little bit is necessary, but not too much. You are overanxious about your children, but you are not

overanxious about my children. You feel so concerned about your children, but you do not think about the children of others. You should be equally concerned about the children of others. You should think about yourself and others alike.

The society which takes care of others is a secure society. If you live in a society where people are always concerned about each other, you will feel very secure. God has blessed you in this life with a beautiful house, a beautiful spouse and beautiful children, but you must care for the rest of the world as well. If you want to change society, this is the ultimate philosophy.

GREEN AND PROSPEROUS RIKHIA

"Man's birth, life and death should be ideal and this is possible if we keep a cow. It may not be possible to do so in the cities. That is why I am addressing the people of the villages and towns. I am telling all the villagers, those who are sitting at the back, the mothers over there, that I am a rajarishi, a royal rishi, and I can give cows to you all, but for that you must know how to look after a cow. You must put up a cowshed and teach your family members and children how to look after a cow. We are ready to give you the necessary training. We have a vet with us. I also know animal husbandry; after all, I am the son of a farmer. I have kept hundreds of cows. I can donate a cow to everyone. I am telling you this in earnest.

We will make arrangements for the local water supply as long as I am here. We will do everything for the Rikhia panchayat without depending on the government. We will dig ponds and build lakes; we will bore tube wells and install pumps. We can provide water within a range of ten kilometres. A sannyasin is always very capable. Haven't we also brought down the Ganga and the Yamuna? We have written the shastras, Puranas and epics. In fact, the whole Indian religion was formed by us. Is there a minister who has established a religion? No, it is only the sannyasin, the renunciate, who has founded and perpetuated religion. He lives in a hut, eats only one meal a day, wears only a loincloth, bears heat, cold and hunger. A sannyasin bears everything for his people because he considers them to be his soul.

When I came to Rikhia I had to face a hard and austere life. I have always been an affluent sannyasin; I have lived in opulence. Not even a king or an emperor could have lived as well as I did, but even in the midst of all those comforts I always wondered, 'Is this the ideal life?' These village people are simple and innocent. Many of them do not even have a hut to live in. There is no light in their house, not even a broken bed to sleep on. They are the have-nots; they have nothing. The life of a sannyasin is dedicated to the upliftment of the world. Now just watch me work for you.

Just as I spread yoga throughout the world, I will donate cows to each and every house. Each house will have a water supply. There will be fields to till. I shall see to it that this happens: 'Green Rikhia, prosperous Rikhia.' This is my promise and my pledge to you."

—Swami Satyananda
3 December, 1996

Glossary

Abhisheka – ceremonial bath; consecration
Acharya – teacher
Adharma – not fulfilling one's natural role in life; all that is contrary to dharma
Adi Shankaracharya – a celebrated teacher of Advaita Vedanta who wrote commentaries on the major Upanishads, the *Bhagavad Gita* and *Brahma Sutras*. The founder of the Dashnami tradition of sannyasa, he established four mathas in the four quarters of India. Kanchi Matha, dedicated to Devi, and numerous smaller mathas claim him as founder
Aditya(s) – a god; divinity; the sun as a deity; divine; a noun used for the twelve Adityas, viz. Dhata, Aryama, Mitra, Varuna, Indra, Vivaswan, Tvashta, Vishnu, Anshu, Bhag, Pusha, Parjyanya
Aghora – 'one for whom nothing is abominable'; one who is totally in tune with their nature, having mastered the elements; totally innocent
Agotra – a person who does not belong to one's community of genes
Ajna – the third eye, the command or monitoring psychic/pranic centre, also known as the 'guru chakra'. The centre of individual consciousness, it enables mind to mind communication with the external guru and one's inner self. It represents intuition or the inner pure

awareness engendered by the confluence of ida, pingala and sushumna nadis

Akhara – training ground, particularly for sannyasins

Alakh Bara – 'invisible boundary'; a secluded place which preserves sannyasa traditions

Amar Chitra Katha – comics for children about historical Indian personalities

Amarwa – village in Rikhia panchayat

Ananda – bliss

Anna daan – offering of food

Antahkarana – inner organ, instrument or tool of consciousness; mind, consisting of manas, buddhi, chitta and ahamkara

Anushthana – a resolve to perform a mantra sadhana with absolute discipline for a requisite period of time; a fixed course of sadhana

Anasuya – Dattatreya's mother; see Dattatreya

Arati – rite of worship involving waving of lights with reverence before a deity

Artha – accomplishment; attainment in all spheres of life; material need; wealth

Arya Samaj – a reformist group founded by Swami Dayananda Saraswati, interested in re-establishing vedic customs

Asana – in raja yoga, a physical posture in which one is at ease and in harmony with oneself; the third limb of yoga as described by Sage Patanjali in the *Yoga Sutras*

Asansol – city in the state of West Bengal, India

Atharva Veda – fourth vedic text containing tantric concepts and collection of spells

Atmabhava – feeling for others like for oneself; seeing the atman (soul) equally in all beings

Atma jnana – direct knowledge of the self

Atri – father of Dattatreya

Aurobindo – name of a famous yogi from Pondicherry. He was concerned with the transformative power of yoga on all levels of the human being

Avatara – God in tangible form; incarnation of God

Ayodhya – birthplace of Lord Rama
Ayurveda – science of health or medicine, the vedic system of medical diagnosis and treatment
Barfi – Indian sweet
Basukinath – temple dedicated to Lord Shiva near Deoghar
Batasha – a sweet
Batuk – young boy, celibate
Bhagavad Gita – 'divine song', Lord Krishna's discourse to Arjuna delivered on the battlefield of Kurukshetra during the great Mahabharata war. It is one of the source books of Hindu philosophy, containing the essence of the Upanishads and yoga
Bhartrihari – famous grammarian and poet of ancient India
Bhava – feelings; emotions; love; condition; state, inclination or disposition of mind
Bhava samadhi – absorption in meditation due to emotional cause e.g. kirtan; superconscious state of existence attained by intense emotion
Bhavani – goddess in-charge of all the power and energy
Bhet – the art of giving and receiving
Bhiksha – alms; offerings
Bhishma – grand uncle of the Pandavas
Bhoga – experience and craving for pleasure; enjoyment, delight; object of pleasure
Bholenath/Bhole – Swami Satyananda's (dog) companion during his panchagni sadhana; affectionately known as Bhole
Bhoomi – ground, the earth, place
Bichiya – toe ring
Bidi – type of cigarette
Bigha – a measure of land
Bilaspur – Indian city in the state of Chhattisgarh
Brahmin – of the priestly caste; a person whose life is dedicated to the study of the Vedas and dispensation of the knowledge of Brahman and is thus qualified to act as a priest in vedic rituals; one of the four guilds or divisions of the caste system in India

Brihadaranyaka – literally 'the great teaching from the forest'; name of an Upanishad from the *Shatapatha Brahmana* of the *Yajurveda*. It discusses the identity of the individual atma (soul) in relation to the universal self, different modes of worship, religion and meditation
Brinjal – a green vegetable, also known as lady's fingers
Chakravarti – a monarch
Chakravarti samrat – the great monarch
Chandi – a manifestation of Durga, Chandi is invincible in battle against demonic forces
Chapatti or **roti** – a flat, round bread
Chappals – shoes; sandals
Chaturmas – the four months of the monsoon traditionally used for sadhana. This auspicious period begins on the day after the full moon of Ashada (Guru Poornima) and comprises the lunar months of Shravana, Bhadrapada, Ashwina and Kartika
Chaura – broad; a platform
Chhat – sixth day after the dark night of moon in October-November according to the lunar Indian calendar on which a festival dedicated to the sun god is observed, mainly in the state of Bihar
Chitabhoomi – cremation ground, particularly Sati's cremation ground
Chitragupta – the celestial record keeper
Choli – scarf
Crore – ten million
Daan – gift, donation; offering; unconditional giving
Dahej or **daibhag** – the daughter's right of inheritance to her parents' property; commonly, the wealth that a woman carries with her after marriage
Dahi-chura – curd and flattened rice
Dakshina – offering, usually to guru
Darshan – a glimpse, seeing, observing; sight, vision; revelations or truths seen in a higher state of consciousness

Dattatreya – an ancient sage who learned from twenty-four gurus, the son of Atri and Anasuya, considered to have been an incarnation of Brahma, Vishnu and Shiva

Daya – sympathy, pity, tenderness, compassion

Deenabandhu – friend to the unfortunate

Deoghar – literally means 'home of the gods'; city in India eleven kilometres from Rikhia

Devakinandan – son of Devaki, Lord Krishna

Devata – form of divine dignity or power; divine being representing the higher state of evolution; illumined form; divinity, deity

Devi – female deity, goddess; name of Durga, Saraswati and others

Dhanbad – city in India in the state of Jharkhand

Dharma – the natural role we play in life; ethical law; duty; the laws or fundamental support of life; usage, practice, custom; religion; virtue, righteousness, good work

Dhoti – cloth worn around the waist

Diwali – festival of lights in India

Diya or **deepak** – small lamp

Dudhahari – a person whose diet is only milk

Durga – remover of difficulties, the beautiful goddess who slays the difficult and even impossible enemies and rides the lion or tiger; a name of the wife of Shiva; the higher state of human consciousness and evolution

Durga Saptashati – part of the Puranic literature which tells the story of Durga's creation from the combined power (shakti) of the gods so that she could overcome all enemies in battle. It tells of her glories and victories over the demonic forces and forms part of the *Devi Mahatmya* of the *Markandeya Purana*

Duryodhana – one of the Kaurava brothers

Dussehra – the tenth day of the bright half of the month of Ashwin in the lunar Indian calendar, when the demon king Ravana was slain by Lord Rama, celebrated across India by burning effigies of Ravana

Dwapara period – the third aeon of the world, consisting of 864,000 years according to *Surya Siddhanta*

Dwiragaman – second arrival, a special ceremony when a bride goes to her husband's home after marriage to stay

Ekadashi – eleventh day of the lunar fortnight, a time when mantra chanting and dietary restraint are held to be beneficial

Gamhar – name of a tree

Ganesha – name of the auspicious, elephant-headed deity, son of Shiva and Parvati

Gangotri – source of the Ganga River

Gargi – female sage whose questions and debates are recorded in *Brihadaranyaka Upanishad*

Gayatri – a vedic metre of twenty-four syllables; a most famous and sacred mantra suitable for everyone, repeated by every person of the priestly caste (brahmin) at the time of their morning and evening devotion (sandhya); vedic goddess, mother of the Vedas; female counterpart of the Sun

Gerudharis – those dressed in the colour geru, sannyasins

Gharwali – ruler of the home

Gobar – cow dung

Gobar gas – cow dung produced combustible gas, used for cooking, lighting, etc.

Gopala – another name of Krishna, particularly referring to his childhood days in the countryside of Vrindavan

Goshala – cowshed

Gotra – family race, family name; spiritual lineage

Goytha – cow dung cake used as fuel

Granthi – psychic knot; the three granthis on the sushumna nadi hinder the upward passage of kundalini, viz. brahma granthi, vishnu granthi and rudra granthi

Griha lakshmi – the goddess of the house, wife

Grihastha – the second stage of life according to the ancient vedic ashrama tradition, household or married life from twenty-five to fifty years of age

Guna – quality; subordinate or constituent part; attribute, characteristic or property of all creation

Guru Poornima – holy day for worship of guru or spiritual teacher when the disciple receives blessings from the guru. It is celebrated on the full moon of the lunar month of Ashada, and Chaturmas sadhana begins the next day

Gurukul – educational system of ancient India, where children lived in the ashram or family of the guru and were taught a comprehensive syllabus for life by the guru, including the Vedangas

Halwa – Indian sweet

Hanuman – name of a powerful monkey chief. He possessed extraordinary strength and powers which he manifested on several critical occasions on behalf of Sri Rama, the Lord of his heart. He was the chief minister of Rama's allied king Sugreeva, and played a very important part in the great war at Lanka

Hanuman Chalisa – Hymn in praise of Hanuman

Haridwar – holy town at the foothills of the Himalayas

Harish Chandra – an ancient Indian king known for his truthfulness

Havan – fire ritual

Holi – festival of colours or spring festival; beginning of the new year according to one of the Indian almanacs

Ishta deva – personal deity, one's favourite god, one's tutelary deity, the aspect of God which is dear to one

Ishta mantra – mantra of the chosen deity

Ishwarchand Vidyasagar – famous Indian personality

Jagadguru – guru of all gurus

Jala – water

Janaka – name of a famous king of Videha or Mithila, who was the foster-father of Sita. He was remarkable for his great knowledge, good works and holiness

Japa – to rotate or repeat continuously without a break; repetition of a mantra or name of God

Jhoola – cradle or swing

Jhoolan – cradle or swing ceremony

Jhumaka – long, dangling earrings

Jivatma – the individual or personal soul

Jnana – knowing, understanding; consciousness, cognizance; higher knowledge derived from meditation or from inner experience; wisdom; the organ of intelligence, sense, intellect

Jnana chakshu – literally the 'eye of wisdom' or intelligence, the mind's eye; the third eye; immediate vision of reality

Jyotirlingam – natural oval-shaped stone worshipped as Lord Shiva, there are twelve jyotirlingams worshipped in different parts of India; symbol of pure consciousness; the effulgent shivalingam in sahasrara symbolizing the illumined state of consciousness; induces concentration of mind

Kabir – a 15th century mystic and poet

Kadhi – a curry made of chickpea flour and yoghurt

Kailash – holy mountain in Tibet, believed to be the home of Shiva

Kaivalya – final liberation; that state of consciousness which is beyond duality

Kali – goddess of destruction and wife of Lord Shiva; epithet of Parvati or Durga; divine mother; primal manifestation of Shakti who destroys time, space and object (as well as ignorance)

Kali Yuga – the age of Kali, which lasts 432,000 years and is the fourth and current era (yuga) of the world now more than 5,000 years old, the 'iron' age, dark, evil, difficult and full of strife

Kama – emotional need for fulfilment; wish, object of desire

Kamakhya – most powerful and famous tantric seat of Devi in the Indian state of Assam

Kangan – bracelet

Kanwar – a particular bamboo pole with pots of water from the River Ganga suspended on each end, carried over the shoulder by pilgrims.

Kanwariya – pilgrim who carries the kanwar; guest of Shiva

Kanya – young girl, virgin

Kanya Kumari – Cape Camorin, a place of pilgrimage dedicated to the Virgin Goddess, at the tip of South India in the state of Tamil Nadu

Karka Sankranti – summer solstice, 16th July, when the sun enters the sign of Cancer

Karna – unacknowledged son of Kunti and Surya (the sun god), who nevertheless became famous for his courage, nobility, loyalty and generosity. He was a celebrated warrior on the side of the Kauravas in the *Mahabharata*, but was finally placed in an untenable position when Lord Krishna and his mother explained that Arjuna and the Pandavas were actually his brothers

Karobari – caretaker

Kartika – eighth lunar month of the Hindu almanac, corresponding to October/November and deemed auspicious for sadhana

Kaunteya – son of Kunti (mother of the Pandavas), an epithet for Arjuna

Kaushalya – mother of Lord Rama

Kirtan – singing of God's name; practice in which a group of people sing a collection of mantras

Kripa – blessing; grace; mercy

Kshatriya – the kingly or warrior caste, one of the four divisions of the caste system in India; one who protects others from injury

Kula – family, lineage

Kula devata – family deity

Kumbha Mela – huge bathing festival held at four auspicious places on the Ganga River (Ganges) every twelve years. The pot (kumbha) of nectar (amrit) that was found after churning the ocean ans was placed on earth in four places, viz. Nasik, Ujjain, Haridwar and Allahabad (the modern name for Prayag). Millions of devotees attend the gatherings and the heads of the sannyasa traditions meet

Kundalini – the primordial cosmic energy located in the individual

Kutir – small hut; simple dwelling
Laddoo – sweet ball
Lakh – a hundred thousand
Lakshmi – goddess in-charge of all the wealth in the world
Langoti – loin cloth
Lanka – name of the island residence of Ravana, presently called Sri Lanka
Lehenga – a long, wide skirt
Linga – mark, sign, characteristic; idol of Shiva; a naturally formed oval stone; often means the Shivalingam, an archetypal symbol
Loka – plane of existence, dimension
Lokamanya Tilak – famous Indian personality
Lord Mrityunjaya – one who is victorious over death; a form of Shiva
Madhuri Dixit – Bollywood actress
Mahabharata – epic of ancient India said to be composed by Rishi Veda Vyasa, involving the history and consequences of the great battle between the Kaurava and Pandava princes. It describes the rivalries and contests of the five sons of Pandu (the Pandavas) and the hundred sons of Dhritarashtra (the Kauravas). It consists of eighteen sections and the *Bhagavad Gita* is a part of it
Mahamantra – 'great mantra'; *Hare Rama Hare Rama Rama Rama Hare Hare; Hare Krishna Hare Krishna Krishna Krishna Hare Hare*
Mahamrityunjaya – 'the great one who is victorious over death'; a form of Shiva
Maharishi – 'great seer'; a great sage or saint; singer of vedic hymns
Mahatma – 'great soul'; used with reference to a person who has destroyed the ego and realized the self as one with all; high-souled, high-minded, magnanimous, noble; supreme consciousness, supreme spirit
Mahua – name of a tree
Maihar – a place of pilgrimage dedicated to Devi Sharada in the central state of Madhya Pradesh in India

Makar Sankranti – the day on which the sun crosses the equator on its northward passage – 14th or 15th January

Mala – wreath, garland, necklace; rosary; in yoga a mala may be made of beads of various substances such as tulsi, rudraksha, sandalwood, sphatika (crystal). One function is to aid mantra repetition

Mandir – a temple or place of worship

Mangalasutra – an auspicious thread, necklace made of gold, some inlaid with diamonds, pearls and precious stones. Traditional necklace of black pearl beads which the husband gives to the wife during the marriage ceremony

Mansarovar – lake near Mount Kailash in Tibet

Margasheersha – ninth lunar month according to the Hindu almanac, corresponding to November/December

Marwari – of the region of Marwar in Rajasthan

Matribhoomi – motherland

Matrivansha – maternal lineage

Maya – cause of the phenomenal world; partial understanding; wrong or false notions about self-identity; power of creation; illusive power

Mela – fete or festival

Mithila – capital of the ancient kingdom of Videha, ruled by King Janaka, the father of Sita

Mohammed – prophet of the Islamic religion

Mohanpur – village near Rikhia

Moksha – liberation, freedom, release; state of existence; in yoga, final emancipation, liberation from the wheel of births and deaths, the aim of yogic practices

Mouna – silence; measured silence, remaining silent for a specified span of time

Mukhia – village chief

Muni – one who contemplates; one who maintains silence or stillness of mind; sage; ascetic

Naam – name and form

Naamkaran – naming ceremony

Nadi – psychic current; flow of energy. *Hatha Yoga Pradipika* and *Shiva Swarodaya* posit 72,000 nadis in the human body, of which three are most important

Naga – militant sannyasa sect, an order of sadhus distinguishable by their nakedness

Nakshatra – phase of the moon

Namaskara – salutation

Narada – name of a celebrated devarishi; one of the ten mentally conceived sons of Brahma, said to have sprung from his thigh. He is represented as a messenger from the gods who is fond of promoting discord amongst gods and humankind. Supposedly the inventor of the lute or veena and also the author of the *Narada Bhakti Sutras*

Narayana – 'companion of man', epithet of Vishnu, the supporter of life; the life forces of all lives; name of an ancient sage said to be a companion of Nara

Nasha – intoxication

Nasik – see Kumbha Mela

Nathani – nose ring

Navaratri – literally 'nine night sadhana', a special sadhana done for nine days twice a year, once during the month of Chaitra, corresponding to March/April and once during Ashwin, corresponding to September/October

Nawadih – village near Rikhiapeeth

Neem – name of a tree well-known for its medicinal purposes

Neetishatak – a text by Sage Bhartrihari

Nigrah – forbearance and fortitude

Nirakara – without form, formless, devoid of form; unmanifest

Nirguna – without quality or attribute, formless

Nirvikalpa Samadhi – state in which the mind ceases to function and only pure consciousness remains, revealing itself to itself and there is no object of the mind; superconscious state where mental modifications cease to exist, resulting in transcendence of the manifest world

Nishkama seva – karma yoga or selfless work, action without desire for fruit and with a feeling for it in one's heart
Panchami – the fifth day of the lunar calendar
Panchanga – current astrological calendar (almanac) which gives daily astrological readings
Panchayat – the village community; county
Pandas – priests
Pandit – priest; learned man; scholar; man of wisdom
Paneer – cottage cheese
Paniya Pagar – village immediately neighbouring Rikhiapeeth
Para – superior, highest, greatest
Paramahamsa – literally 'supreme swan', a swan is reputed to be able to separate milk from water, that is, reality from unreality; one who controls or subdues their passions; a sage, an ascetic; title of a person in the fourth stage of consciousness
Paramatma – cosmic soul or consciousness, Supreme Self; the atma (self or soul) of the entire universe, of the individual as well as of the cosmos; liberated state of the inner self
Pashmina shawl – fine woollen shawl
Pashupatinath – famous Shiva temple in Nepal
Patra daan – offering of vessels
Puwal – straw
Peeth – abode; place; seat
Pooja – honour, respect; rites; worship
Poori – fried bread
Pradhan – the chief
Prajna – knowledge with awareness; awareness of the one without a second
Prakriti – individual nature; manifest and unmanifest nature; cosmic energy; the active principle of manifest energy; nature or primordial matter (source of the universe)
Pranayama – a series of techniques using the breath to control the flow of prana within the body
Prasad – grace, blessed gift or object, something full of grace

Pravara – a sage who is supposed to be the progenitor of a family; family; descendant
Prayaschitta – type of austerity; atonement for one's acts of unawareness during all births
Pujari – officiating priest at a religious ceremony
Pune – city in the state of Maharashtra, India
Purana – past event; ancient, old; name of a class of sacred texts believed to be composed by Rishi Vyasa – eighteen ancient texts containing the earliest mythology of the tantric and vedic traditions
Purascharana – observance consisting of the repetition of a mantra
Puri – town, city
Raghunath – a name of Lord Rama
Raja Rama Mohan Roy – a famous Indian personality
Rajarishi – royal sage; philosopher king; a rishi who is a kshatriya (warrior)
Rajasooya Yajna – sacrifice (yajna) of large dimensions performed by an emperor
Rajnandgaon – city in the state of Madhya Pradesh, India
Rajas – one of the three constituent qualities (gunas) of nature (prakriti) and all matter; dynamism; state of activity; creativity combined with full ego involvement; emotion; restlessness; oscillation; as a personality trait it is expressed by the desire to dominate
Ram Naam Aradhana – worship of Lord Rama by chanting his name; month-long program held at Rikhiapeeth in 1996 in praise of Lord Rama
Rama – the hero of the epics *Ramayana* and *Ramacharitamanas*, the seventh incarnation of Vishnu as the son of Dasharatha and Kaushalya and the most dutiful disciple of Vishwamitra. He married Sita after he performed the wonderful feat of bending Shiva's bow
Ramacharitamanas – a version of the *Ramayana* written in a Hindi dialect by Tulsidas
Ramakrishna – a paramahamsa who worshipped Mother Kali; lived at Dakshineshwar near Kolkata

Ramayana – literally 'the path of Rama', one of the most famous ancient Indian epics, composed by Valmiki, containing about 24,000 verses in seven chapters
Ranade – famous Indian personality
Ravana – the ten-headed demon king of Lanka, who kidnapped Sita and was subsequently slain by Rama. His ten heads symbolize attachment to phenomenal reality via the five jnanendriyas and the five karmendriyas
Rickshaw – a small two-wheeled, hooded carriage drawn by a man or powered by a man on a bicycle
Rishi – ascetic, anchorite, seer; realized sage; one who contemplates or meditates on the self; one who experiences other dimensions
Ritambhara – full of experience; cosmic harmony
Sadhana – spiritual practice or discipline performed regularly for the attainment of inner experience and self-realization
Sadhu – good, virtuous or holy person; sage, saint
Sakara – with form; manifest
Sakhi – female attendant to bride at the time of marriage
Samrat – king
Samskara – impression on the memory of all patterns and mental impressions of the past, which remain unnoticed in the mind, yet set up impulses and trains of thought; unconscious memories; impressions that do not fit into the known categories of our present personality; sixteen traditional rituals marking different stages in life observed in Hindu culture in a process of purification undergone by the soul after arrival in the body of a human being; process of consecration performed on an item of oblation
Sandesh – Indian sweet made from milk
Sandhya – spiritual practice required to be practised by a student after the upanayana samskara at three conjunction times of dawn, noon and dusk
Sankalpa – will, volition, positive resolve; purpose, aim, intention

Sankalpa shakti – willpower
Sannyasa – dedication; complete renunciation of the world, its possessions and attachments; abandonment of the temporal; the six stages of sannyasa life are known as kutichaka, bahudaka, hamsa, paramahamsa, turiyateeta and avadhuta; the fourth of four stations (ashramas) in the vedic concept of a full life
Sannyasin – one who has taken sannyasa initiation; a yogi; one who is not dependent on the results of action
Santhal – native tribe of the region of Deoghar and surrounding areas
Saraswati – goddess in-charge of all the arts and learning
Sarovar – reservoir
Sat Chandi Mahayajna – a powerful fire sacrifice performed in honour of Chandi during which the Durga Saptashati is chanted one hundred times over several days
Sat karma – selfless or divine karma
Satsang – the holy company of sadhus and sannyasins
Saundarya Lahari – ode to Shakti reputedly composed by Adi Shankaracharya
Savikalpa samadhi – a kind of samadhi in which the mind still retains its material impressions, distinctions such as that between subject and object, or of the knower and the known
Seer – seer of the subtle essence of things; one who has developed the subtle inner eye; a wise person; a sage
Seva – service; offering oneself wholly for His cause; doing work for the Lord
Shaiva – those who worship Shiva as the supreme reality
Shakti – cosmic energy; primal energy; manifest consciousness; strength, energy; the female aspect of creation and divinity; power that is eternal and supreme and of the nature of consciousness; counterpart of Shiva; in Hindu mythology Shakti is often symbolized as a divine woman
Shakti peethas – important places for worship of Shakti

Shakti tantra – tantric sect extolling the Goddess as the Supreme Being

Shaktipat – higher energy or experience transmitted by the guru to a worthy disciple; descent of power through worship (upasana)

Shankaracharya – originally the name of a celebrated teacher of the Advaita Vedanta philosophy, acclaimed as the author of the commentary (bhashya) on the *Brahma Sutras* and a large number of other works. He was the enlightened sage who is said to have established the Dashnami order of sannyasa and became the first or Adi 'Shankaracharya', which is an honorary title for pontiffs of the matha of that tradition

Shanti – peace, calmness, tranquillity, quiet

Shantiniketan – a place of higher learning in verdant surroundings near Kolkata created by Rabindranath Tagore

Shesham – teak tree

Shiva Purana – collection of six ancient scriptures that tell the story of Shiva.

Shivalingam – black oval-shaped stone (those occurring naturally in the Narmada river are especially revered); symbol of Lord Shiva; symbol of consciousness

Shramjeevi – the working class

Shravan – fifth lunar month according to the Hindu almanac, corresponding to July/August

Shringara – adornment

Shudra – one of the four varnas or divisions of the caste system in India; one with a service-oriented tendency of mind or one engaged in such a profession

Shukla Panchami – the fifth day of the bright fortnight

Siddha – accomplished soul particularly characterized by spiritual attainments (siddhis)

Siddhi – spiritual attainment

Sita – the name of the daughter of Janaka and the wife of Rama. Sita is the heroine of the epic *Ramayana*

Smashan – cremation ground

Smriti – memory; one of the five vrittis listed in Sage Patanjali's *Yoga Sutras*; tradition, law, the body of traditional or memorial law; canon; vedic texts transmitted by memory; a class of works called dharma shastra handed down by tradition
Solah shringara – the sixteen items of beautification
Sthan – place, locality, region
Streedhanam – the wealth that belongs to a woman
Sudarshan chakra – Shiva's ultimate weapon; the name of the discus of Lord Vishnu
Suhaag – auspicious
Sultanganj – city on the Ganga River about one hundred kilometres from Deoghar
Taittiriya Upanishad – an Upanishad in the form of a lesson to a student. The first chapter, *Shiksha Valli*, is on right education and the second, *Ananda Valli*, is on bliss
Tamo guna – one of the three constituent qualities (gunas) of nature (prakriti) and all matter; inertia, stability, stillness; ignorance, darkness
Tantra – most ancient universal science and culture which deals with the transition of human nature from the present level of evolution and understanding to a transcendental level of knowledge, experience and awareness
Tapas – austerity; 'that which generates heat'
Tapasvi – ascetic, one who practises austerity or penance
Tapovanam – forest suitable for tapas.
Tattwa – an element, a primary substance; essence, truth
Teej – a festival of India
Thakur – a chief; a particular caste
Thali – plate
Thela – push cart
Tryambakeshwar – holy place near Nasik containing a temple of Lord Mrityunjaya, Swami Satyananda's ishta devata
Treta Yuga – the second of the four aeons of the world, lasting for 1,296,000 years according to *Suryasiddhanta*; an aeon where goodness is on the increase, leading up to Satya Yuga

Trikuti – eyebrow centre; the space between the two eyebrows; meeting place of the three psychic channels of ida, pingala and sushumna

Tulsi – the holy basil plant of India, sacred to Lord Vishnu and venerated by the Vaishnavas as most divine, she is symbolically married to Shalagrama (a symbol of Lord Vishnu); a herb with many healing capacities; the wood is considered to be very pure and is made into rosary beads (mala) used for mantra japa

Upanayana – literally 'to lead near (to the spiritual teacher)'; the sacred thread ritual, investiture with a sacred thread to initiate participants into sacred learning, one of the samskaras in the vedic tradition

Upanishad – ancient vedic text containing intimate dialogues and discussions between guru and disciple on the nature of the absolute and the path leading towards it; vedantic texts conveyed by ancient sages and seers containing their experiences and teachings on the ultimate reality; the Upanishads are the philosophical portion of the Vedas, the most ancient and sacred literature of the Hindus, dealing with the nature of human beings and the universe. The Upanishads are regarded as the source of the Vedanta, yoga and Samkhya philosophies

Vaishnavite – those who worship Vishnu in the form of Rama, Krishna, Narayana, etc.; the sect that reveres incarnations of Vishnu as the supreme reality and worships God in his supreme form

Vaishya – one of the four divisions of the caste system (varnas) in India, those who specialize in trade or undertake the responsibility of caring for society

Vandana – prayer

Varanasi – one of the most ancient and holiest cities of India, located in the northern state of Uttar Pradesh

Vastra daan – offering of cloth/clothes

Vasu – the soul; the soul of the universe; supreme being; name of Vishnu; the name of Narayana; etymologically, the term means a god who abides in all things and in whom all things abide

Vasuki – name of a celebrated serpent (Sheshanaga), the king of snakes and said to be a son of Kashyapa

Vedanta – 'the last part of the Vedas'; the Upanishads; Vedanta teaches the ultimate aim and scope of the Vedas. It states that there is one eternal principle (Brahman); philosophy of realization of Brahman; the end of perceivable knowledge, where the mind experiences its own limits and goes beyond them, gaining realization and understanding through that exploration; the school of Hindu thought based primarily on the Upanishads. It upholds the doctrine of either pure non-dualism (Advaita Vedanta) or conditional non-dualism (Vishishta Advaita). Vedanta is also called Uttara Mimamsa; one of the six principal systems of Hindu philosophy (darshanas)

Vedas – the most ancient and sacred literature of the Hindus, dealing with the nature of human beings and the universe. The three Vedas taken collectively, the *Rigveda*, *Sama Veda* and *Yajurveda* are the three original, ancient and most revered Vedas, with the *Atharva Veda* being a relatively later addition

Vindhyachal – mountain range in central India which has many places of pilgrimage

Vishad – unhappiness, dejection, despair

Vishwakarma – name of the architect and engineer of the gods

Vivah Panchami – auspicious day of the marriage of Sita with Lord Rama

Viveka – discrimination

Viveka buddhi – discrimination between right and wrong

Viveka shakti – discriminative force

Vivekananda – well known late 19th century yogi who revitalized yoga and took it to the West

Yajnopaveeta – sacred thread

Yajna – sacrificial rite, offering oblations to the fire

Yajnavalkya – name of sage, author and founder of the *Shukla Yajurveda*; follower of the *Shukla Yajurveda*
Yatri – pilgrim
Yudhishthira – literally 'firm in battle'; name of the first Pandava who was the son of Kunti by the grace of Yama, also known as the king of dharma (Dharmaraja) or the epitome of dharma